PURSUING THE ADDENDA

PURSUING THE ADDENDA

SUPERNATURAL REPORTS FROM THE NATURAL WORLD

JOHN A. KEEL

NEW SAUCERIAN BOOKS, POINT PLEASANT, WEST VIRGINIA

BOOKS BY JOHN A. KEEL

Jadoo!
Operation Trojan Horse
Strange Creatures From Time and Space
Our Haunted Planet
The Mothman Prophecies
The Eighth Tower
Strange Mutants From the 21st Century
Disneyland of the Gods
The Complete Guide to Mysterious Beings
Flying Saucer To the Center of Your Mind
The Outer Limits of the Twilight Zone
Searching For The String
The Great Phonograph In The Sky
The Passionate Percipient: Illusions I Have Known and Loved
The Perspicacious Percipient: How to Investigate UFOs and Other Insane Urges
The Book of Mothman: Everything You Wanted to Know About Reality Distortion But Were Afraid to Ask
I Never Would Have Slept With You If I Had Known You Were A Giant Birdman From Outer Space: Ancient Aliens and Other Mysteries of the Modern Mind
The Invisible Diet: Top-Secret Techniques For Turning Your Miserable Life Completely Around

Pursuing The Addenda

ISBN-13: 978-0692737064

ISBN-10: 0692737065

PUBLISHED BY: New Saucerian Books – Point Pleasant, West Virginia

CONTENTS

PUBLISHER'S NOTE

This book rounds out a triple trilogy of Keel books, all nine of which were a pleasure to edit. The first trilogy, *Flying Saucer to the Center of Your Mind*, *The Outer Limits of the Twilight Zone*, and *Searching For the String*, is an overview of Forteana and ufology, giving the reader a fresh perspective on the history and progress of research in those areas.

The Great Phonograph in the Sky, *The Passionate Percipient: Illusions I Have Known and Loved*, and *The Perspicacious Percipient: How to Investigate UFOs and Other Insane Urges*, the second set, goes into more detail, examining how the physical sciences (physics, engineering, medicine, etc.) can help explain unusual phenomena, or at least point the way to a better understanding.

The third trilogy, *The Book of Mothman: Everything You Ever Wanted to Know About Reality Distortion But Were Afraid to Ask*, *I Never Would Have Slept With You If I Had Known You Were A Giant Birdman From Outer Space: Ancient Aliens and Other Mysteries of the Modern Mind*, and *Pursuing the Addenda: Supernatural Reports From the Natural World* bring the reader full circle, by providing a broad, "cosmic" view, explaining how many Fortean events may be related – a relationship that is as old as the planet and perhaps the universe.

Keel wrote many of the articles before you for *Pursuit* magazine, the quarterly journal of the Society For the Investigation of the Unexplained (SITU), a non-profit research organization founded by Ivan Sanderson, the noted British zoologist, on August 25, 1965.

The Society was registered with the Warren County, New Jersey County Clerk and the State of New Jersey, and was geared toward scientists on both sides of the Atlantic, for "the acquisition, investigation, and dissemination of information on reports of all tangible items in the fields of chemistry, astronomy, geology, biology and anthropology that are not readily explained."

For well over three decades, it was the leading organization pursuing research on anomalous phenomena of the kind usually associated with Charles Fort. It encouraged fieldwork and on-the-spot investigation by offering advice, helping to raise funds, and arranging contacts for members who planned field trips and expeditions. Fieldwork and research were peer-reviewed by a panel of twenty accredited scientists.

The Society maintained information files of original material, a map collection, and a specialized library. Sanderson built a concrete bunker on the property to house the materials, which were so vast that it became notorious as the "holy grail" of Forteana.

Sadly, as Sanderson was dying of cancer in 1973, the bunker was raided by an unknown group of people, who after pretending to browse, filled up several cars and trucks with files and drove off, never to be seen again.

According to researcher Loren Coleman, "the 'borrowed' books and files were never returned. Ivan Sanderson's concrete building that he had built on his land, specifically to house his decades of materials, was legendary. It was filled to overflowing with his priceless library."

Such was the state of things until March 20, 2011, when Michael D. Swords, on his blog *The Big Story*, announced that *he* was in possession of the missing Sanderson files!

Swords, a retired professor of Natural Science at Western Michigan University, explained that the files had first fallen under the "ownership/stewardship of a wonderfully fine fellow, absolutely dedicated to the preservation of anomalistic archival methods, Dr. John Reed of the Society For Scientific Exploration (SSE)."

As Reed began getting too old to care for the collection, Swords rushed to the rescue and "saved" the materials, which apparently fill a 26-foot U-haul trailer, and are currently located at 818 South Park St., Kalamazoo, Michigan. According to Swords, one can "request to browse the files at any time," by simply emailing him.

One wonders how well that system works, especially if one is a fan of John Keel. Swords has long been a member of the "conservative" or "skeptical" ufological crowd, prone to promoting the writings of "official" oracles like Keyhoe, Hynek, Ruppelt, Jacobs, Randle, etc. – whom Keel routinely skewered. (Keel called out the SSE, CSICOP, MUFON/CUFOS crowd – to which Swords belonged – several times, for suppressing information and "engaging in a battle with new ideas.")

It would have been in the interest of the SSE, a rival group also claiming to be "scientific," to suppress the Sanderson files, which had ballooned due to Keel's call for more "data, data, data." Without data, Keel's interdimensional or 4-D thesis could be quashed, leaving the antigravity field free to be exploited, away from prying eyes and public awareness, by defense contractors – the "buddies" of the skeptics.

Luckily, after Ivan's death, his wife gathered what was left of his personal papers (which had been kept in safer locations) and donated them to the American Philosophical Society Library in Philadelphia. Until the "missing" Sanderson files, now in the hands of Michael Swords, are donated to a university or library with regular working hours, ensuring public access, we can't yet say that the files weren't purloined outright.

John Keel took over the leadership of the Society, and the journal, after Sanderson died. Prior to that, Keel had worked with Sabina Sanderson, Ivan's wife, to edit, proofread, print, and distribute *Pursuit*, which ran on a shoestring budget, and to organize the voluminous files that would later be appropriated by the SSE.

After Keel's traumatic experiences with Men in Black, UFOs, and various entities in West Virginia and New York during the years 1966 to 1968, he basically went into hiding on the Sanderson farm, on the slopes of the Allegheny Mountains near Blairstown, New Jersey. He wrote much of his breakthrough book, *Operation Trojan Horse*, at the farm, and was a frequent lodger there until 1973, when he began typing out *The Mothman Prophecies* and *The Eighth Tower*, considered by some to be his best books.

Despite one's opinions of the ranking of those works, they are certainly a little different than Keel's previous books, in that they were not taken directly from earlier Keel articles, written for magazines like *Fate*, *True*, and *Saga* (the latter being the basis for many of the compilations we have done). While his later works examined much of the same material he had already covered, the insights came from more unexpected angles, and generally seemed more mature and open-ended.

Pursuing the Addenda, coming as it did on the heels of Mothman, can thus be considered a bridge between the two eras in Keel's life – before Mothman (when he was devising a "unified theory" to explain the phenomena, based on reports), and after Mothman (when he was able to incorporate many new, hard-won realizations, based on personal experience and reflection).

There are no easy answers in this field, so it is often best to say that you simply "don't know." Keel could admit this, but he also had an encyclopedic mind, and could certainly argue for a "solution" better than most others. He was obviously considered a threat by some (usually those of a religious, right-wing, or "former military" bent), particularly during this "transitional" phase, so it is likely there is something in these pages that "they" don't want you to know.

-Andy Colvin

EDITOR'S NOTE

What Charles Fort called "acceptance" has changed drastically. We speak, of course, of the attitude to reality of philosophers with scientific training.

As we have repeatedly observed, humanity ran on belief until the incident at Hiroshima. Since then, it has been forced to re-orientate its entire outlook to conform to reality. It's not that "God" died that day, as so many assert; but rather that the concept of an infinitely competent and benign power then literally dropped dead.

What we euphemistically call "Nature" – another way of saying "Reality" – is not benign. It is, from our human way of thinking, infinitely cruel and gruesomely efficient.

All manner of people who have truly studied reality through realistic (i.e., "scientific") channels have ultimately been forced to accept the possibility of other realities – at least if they managed to remain intellectually honest.

Ever more properly trained minds of a philosophical turn, and an extraordinary number of pure technologists, have cast off the shackles of the "old" mechanics, for the very simple reason that their own discoveries have demonstrated, without a doubt, that there are not only other "mechanics," but also other worlds of both logic and reality.

As you turn the pages John Keel has allotted to this business, you will see what I mean. John Keel is not the first but the last (or most recent) thinker to express cogent opinions on this "Reality" of ours, which has exercised the minds and deep attention of all religions for centuries, and of most governments, many "scientists," and hosts of others.

To the prior acceptance of these new concepts there have been two roadblocks: 1) the old-time scientists; and 2) the religionists and other mystics – the occultists, psychic mediums, and Spiritualists. What both parties have failed to realize is that there is a "third world," which is just as real as our mechanical-physical one. But it does not run on our laws, principles, or even logic. Moreover, it is not part of the "spiritual world."

If you want to know what it is – and you had better get with it if you want to survive – then devour books like this one by Keel. They point to pragmatic evidence – which science now must accept – of the existence of another (or many other) existence(s), interwoven with ours, with which we are beginning to make contact through our technology, bringing a new and better understanding of the operation and scope of what we call "mind."

Not only have scientists like J. Allen Hynek and Jacques Vallee come into agreement with Keel; there are now many others, including prominent physicists and such enormous hegemonies as the Roman Catholic Church and several federal governments.

Keel's basic theme is that UFOs and a whole gamut of other constantly reported mysteries are not extraterrestrial (per se), but what he calls "ultra-terrestrial," meaning that they emanate from this "other world" that exists alongside our own.

Strange, indeed, that we once again come back to Charles Fort who, not so long ago, suggested that we might be nothing but the "property" of some other, if not higher, intelligence, which actually controls us in every respect – even our evolution.

Is this not what the new understanding and "acceptance" implies?

-Ivan T. Sanderson

CHAPTER 1

THE CURRENT STATUS OF UFOLOGY – JANUARY 1969

Whatever the findings of the Condon Committee may be – and its report should be released before this issue reaches you – we are currently living through a most interesting period, not only of ufological history, but also of intellectual development as a whole. In fact, we should endeavor to grasp the real significance of current events in this field and their overall impact on our thinking.

This is actually as near a renaissance as humanity has undergone since the great awakening five hundred years ago. Innumerable new discoveries made by the exercise of scientific methodology have contributed to this, but regardless of whether it is all fact or fancy, it is ufology that must be credited with having forced the breakthrough; and credit for this is due to a small band of dedicated specialists in this field.

We are sick of the picayune squabbles of the various parties to this enquiry, ranging as they do from starry-eyed mystics to what are still considered "renegade" scientists, and we do not agree wholeheartedly with any of them.

Nonetheless, all have contributed something to the more general and much greater cause of intellectual stimulation and worthwhile speculation. Even if the whole business of "flying saucers," "little green men," official bungling, hot air inversions, swamp gases, and plasma balls are nothing more than illusory, the fact remains that their advocates have collectively implemented Archimedes' ancient plea – namely, "Give me a lever big enough and I will move the world."

Practically speaking, these assorted types have, by their very persistence, forced both scholars and the general public to face up to the previously unsuspected possibilities of existence. Their efforts are, collectively, every bit as revolutionary as those of Galileo, Keppler, Herschel, Bacon, Newton, and such ilk; for, what they have done is to force twentieth-century established thinking into new channels.

By this, we mean that they have, by their very persistence, shoved everybody, and notably sciencedom, into at least admitting that there could be more to existence than has previously met their eyes.

Ufology itself is passing through a most interesting phase, and this on several counts. Most significant is the undeniable fact that, even if it has not become wholly respectable, it is being taken seriously and discussed very widely in both intellectual and technological circles.

Who, even among ufologists, ever hoped, a decade ago, to see such exercises as the Condon Committee, Congressional hearings, and papers on the subject read before such august and even hidebound organizations as the Institute of Electrical and Electronic Engineers, the American Astronautical Society, the American Society of Mechanical Engineers; and articles and letters by scientists in such publications as *Science*, *Look*, *The Saturday Review*, *Time*, and so forth, or, above all, in newspapers of such conservatism as *The London Times* and *The New York Times*?

The plain and undeniable fact is that as yet unexplained and/or unidentified objects reportedly observed in the sky (and more especially, landing on the earth, or diving into oceans, seas, lakes, and even rivers) simply will not go away.

A Gallup poll startled even the "believers" when it blandly stated that millions of Americans claim to have observed such things, and that several million more stated they knew people – whom they trust – who say they have seen them; and that still greater numbers were willing to state that they believe such things do exist.

Even the scientific establishment can't buck this tide of belief.

The actual status of ufology itself is currently more than ambiguous. For all the public statements, interest by scientists, official denials, and even the expressions of ufologists themselves, there is a coverup.

Despite the constant refrain that we really cannot go any further, at present, because we "haven't got one," there are positively swarms of "authorities" talking glibly about the nature of "specimens" that have been obtained, and the incomprehensible items that have been found in them.

Of living or robotic entities among these items, nothing is said or even offered; this is possibly because these glib informers are all engineers or other technologists, and none are biologists. There is, however, just as much reason to suppose or assume that we have got some UFOs, as there is to accept the visual reports of them or even their very existence.

If nothing else were needed to demonstrate this possibility, the mere catalogue of cases (wherein the armed services or other official outfits have swooped upon areas in which UFOs have been reported to have landed, and cordoned them off) ought to give anybody pause.

And that these cases are not mere hearsay or irresponsible newspaper coverage is demonstrable by the fact that a very high percentage of them have been confirmed by police and other sheriffs, and not infrequently on the air. (We have transcripts on tape of several of these.)

If all such reports that were so swooped upon turned out to be false alarms, officialdom would surely have given up the effort, and the cash outlay to investigate them, long ago. They have not; and, in fact, such activities have grown abundantly over the years.

By the same token, official interest has most noticeably shifted from cataloguing and statistically analyzing funny lights in the sky to interviewing in depth those witnesses, however crazy they may sound, who let it be known that they have stumbled across a UFO on the ground, entered it or observed robotic or living entities coming out of such, or met some "alien" type of humanoid, creature entity, or unknown "animal."

The basic fact to comprehend is that, right or wrong, hallucinated or not, the millions of people who claim to have seen UFOs or encountered them or their occupants have forced scholars to at least a cognizance of the subject.

Further, they have finally persuaded some better thinkers (and even some true scientists) to at least consider the matter and, above all, they have pushed educated humanity, as a whole, into contemplation of new possibilities for existence on or around Earth.

Currently, our culture is writhing in some agony while ingesting this concept, mostly because we have not yet gotten over our age-old egocentric outlook. The very idea that there could be intelligent life elsewhere, or that we are not God's chosen is still abhorrent even to the average communist. Proof positive of either concept, even at this stage, would completely upset our intellectual apple cart. Officialdom knows this only too well.

Change comes slowly, and breakthroughs take a long time to be accepted. A true renaissance in thinking takes over a century. The western world is only a little over two decades into this current one, so don't expect too much too fast.

CHAPTER 2

ON WEDDING RINGS – JANUARY 1969

In our last issue we mentioned, perhaps rather too facetiously, that a SITU member has long collected oddities and enigmas connected with wedding rings. Now, we receive a letter from another member, Mrs. Dulcie Brown, of Fresno, California. It reads in part:

> My wedding ring was silver, with a pretty little band with engraving. I wore it so long that all the engraving wore off, and it was just a plain silver band. Then, it began catching on things and, fearing that my finger might be injured, I took it off and laid it on a sideboard in our Los Angeles home. This was in about 1955.
>
> The wedding ring disappeared. I could not find it anywhere. When we moved from Los Angeles, everything was carefully gone over in the house and garage, and many things disposed of. We were very careful to include just the things we wanted to keep to take with us. But no wedding ring showed up.
>
> Since moving to Fresno, we moved twice and the same thing was done – everything gone over and the dispensable things done away with. No wedding ring. I had forgotten about it.
>
> In 1966, my husband died. This time I really needed to get rid of things. In the garage was a certain box. It had originally been a cigar box – one of those nice little wooden deals with a clasp.
>
> When I was going with my husband back in 1932, I had decorated this box. He had kept it because it was the first thing I had done for him. It contained small articles like nails and screws – little things that one might need. I have opened that box a number of times to take out nails, etc., and have picked through it, item by item.
>
> About a week ago, a young lady came in and asked me for a nail. I opened the little box and on top of everything was my wedding ring!

Sudden disappearances and appearances of material objects is a most troublesome matter. The phenomenon has, until now, been almost universally attributed to some form of self-hypnosis, often involving mystics, occultists, spiritualists, and such other cultists who were asked to aid in the process.

When rational souls claimed such things, simple logic was called upon; namely, that the items had been overlooked or had fallen into a hole; or that a cat or dog had carried them off, or brought them in; or that mice or rats were the culprits (the latter being great collectors).

But such spontaneous appearances have been witnessed now for several decades and under controlled conditions. There is no longer any doubt that inanimate objects "appear," either lobbed or just dropped in. Note the endless cases of stones falling from the sky – a process that has been witnessed by tens of thousands of people, in broad daylight, and with such professional skeptics as police officers and cameramen present.

While the procedure and process may be the same from a physical point of view, there is nonetheless a difference between the appearances of personal artifacts and the appearances of non-artifacts, in that the former appear to be more purposive. Wedding rings are important personal artifacts.

These reports of materializations and dematerializations constitute a natural phenomenon closely parallel to that of UFOs, in that we have nothing concrete by way of explanation, and are still in the collecting stage. There is nothing but reports and a few photographs, and the latter all taken after the event, so that the objects depicted could quite well be nothing but "plants" or hoaxes.

We do have the objects themselves, of course, but then we also have almost as many things, both artifacts and non-artifacts, that have fallen from the sky in the presence of more than enough reliable witnesses.

The real question is: "Exactly what are these objects concrete evidence of?"

CHAPTER 3

CLOSURE FOR DISCLOSURE? – JANUARY 1969

We regret having to allocate this much space to this, but the "Disclosure" subject has, still is, and will continue to be a very vital part of history. It does not matter in the least whether this whole business is real or imaginary. The basic fact is that it exists; and it is a problem that must engage the attention of everybody: politicians (international and national), scientists, religionists, the press, and all other citizens.

We are speaking of what have come to be called UFOs, and whether or not the government has "made contact" with them, and is keeping that fact from you.

We are fully aware of the fact that only a small percentage of you are interested in this business, but certain current events show only too clearly that it is the single most important problem of today – for all of us. Even if the whole thing is based on unreality, the fact remains that the problem is very real.

Unidentified flying objects have persisted in turning up throughout the ages, and with increasing frequency during the past two decades.

The public demanded to know of both officialdom and sciencedom what they were. They got no satisfactory answer. And so, with the latter-day help of the press, they forced the former into taking action (at least in the U.S.). The result was a contract between the USAF's Department of Research and the University of Colorado, which enjoined the latter to conduct a scientific survey of the evidence for the alleged existence of UFOs.

This injunction was accepted in late 1966; and its recipients, under the chairmanship of one Dr. Edward U. Condon, have recently published their findings. If you are interested in such matters, read the book *UFOs? Yes!* by David R. Saunders and R. Roger Harkins.

There is an unwritten but seldom stated maxim along Publishers' Row that, while good reviews may sell books, bad ones almost invariably do so. The corollary to this is even less often mentioned – which is that bad reviews never do any real harm, but too many good ones can kill a potential bestseller.

We are not giving Dr. Saunder's book either a good or a bad review; we are simply reporting on its existence and suggesting that it should be read. But when we come to its counterpart, entitled *The Scientific Study Of Unidentified Flying Objects*, we are only too happy to give it the worst review possible, in the hope that more people will try to read it, because not even a bucolic moron could fail to learn something valuable just from making the effort.

The lesson? The deplorable state into which intellectual integrity has fallen, and the preposterous imbecility of the proponents and practitioners of what the public has been led to believe is – but which most definitely is not – science.

These two books are the outcome of the boondoggle that has become popularly known as the "Condon Committee," set up at a cost of over a half-million dollars, ostensibly to scientifically study the UFO problem. Together, these two books should be required reading for all students entered in or proposing to enter any courses in matters scientific (or technological, for that matter), so that they may know just what they are getting into.

We said in our previous issue that it has been ufology that – sense or nonsense – has caused the world to start truly thinking again. From reading of the outcome of the University of Colorado effort in this sphere, our remarks have perhaps become somewhat prophetic. Unfortunately, what the world has been forced to think about is the exact opposite of that which "sciencedom" intended.

By its deplorable shenanigans and its blathering, hypocritical, sanctimonious report, filled with its endless contradictions and statistical gobbledygook, the Colorado effort should alert everyone to the menace that this sort of cant poses, both intellectually and physically. This whiny singsong is a "crime" against real scientific endeavor and methodology.

CHAPTER 4

NOISY CLOUDS – APRIL 1969

We are always suspicious of a coincidence to the power of only two. Nevertheless, when the time factor crops up on a tight schedule, two outlandish items of a similar nature in a month – on a matter that has not been heard of in over a half-century – become big news. The spatial separation of the two items should be considered:

1. Jacksonville Beach, Florida (AP), 3rd February 1969:

> Hundreds of persons, including Police Chief James Alford, reported strange sounds coming from two clouds.
>
> One man described the sound as like "someone rattling cellophane." A woman said it was more like someone "walking on pebbles."
>
> Alford ordered Capt. Harold Bryan to follow the first cloud. Bryan did so, to the edge of the Atlantic, where the cloud dissipated. The listeners started to go back inside their homes when, they said, another cloud repeated the performance. Bryan also followed it to dissipation over the Atlantic.
>
> Officials at the Mayport Naval Air station said they could offer no explanation; neither could other officials.

2. Miami, Florida (AP), 10th February 1969:

> Flapping, crinkling, crackling clouds were reported over Miami Sunday.
>
> "It sounds like a big bird flapping its wings and trying to get off the ground," said William Ward.
>
> "No, it's more like huge sheets of wax paper being crumpled," said his wife, Charlene.
>
> The clouds were reported over Jacksonville last week, but no one there could explain the sounds; neither could the U.S. Weather Bureau in Miami.

Now, there are various possibilities here. The first is obviously chemi-physical, in that the phenomenon could be due to things of a purely mechanical sort, say "Brownian movement" of ice crystals, or the release of micro-electrostatic exchanges.

But, before we come to further consider these, we should try to clear away an unpleasant suggestions coming from ufologists. They are concerned (rightfully) that a considerable percentage of UFO reports (especially daytime ones) speak of these unidentified flying objects either giving rise to, surrounding themselves by, or otherwise using clouds to make their entrances and getaways – their "appearing" and "disappearing" acts.

Further, there are the UAP, or Unexplained Aerial Phenomena, which are, themselves, diaphanous or cloudlike. The general idea here seems to be that some UFOs either are (to us) "clouds" per se, or they can create and dissipate clouds at will.

Should either suggestion be valid, it would seem likely that some of them might be "rowdy," for either the chemi-physical reasons mentioned above, or for any of a host of others.

The most interesting aspect of these two reports is that a police captain followed the cloud, and witnessed it dissolve or evaporate. This would seem to indicate that it was a special type of cloud, particularly in that it made noises.

Clouds drifting off land and over the ocean very often so dissipate, but this prods our memory of the late Dr. Rolf Alexander from New Zealand, who demonstrated the deliberate dissolution of clouds by "taking thought upon the matter," from the roof of a large department store in Miami in 1960, in the presence of a lot of people, including a police officer and a radio crew (see Walter J. McGraw's *The World of the Paranormal*).

One of our most honored SITU members (Member No. 55) became greatly intrigued with Alexander's experiment, and set about doing a few of his own. He claims to have been able to dissolve clouds!

We must admit that he gave a rather satisfactory demonstration one day in Charleston, West Virginia. He, in company with twelve others of *Pursuit* persuasion, including skeptical geologist Kent Wilcoxson (Member No. 152), were in that state on an archaeological mission.

It had rained torrentially for three days before our arrival, and continued to do so all night. Purely kiddingly, we asked Member No. 55 to do something about it.

He proceeded directly onto a verandah, alone, for a time and – lo and behold – a large break appeared in the dense dark overcast, precisely over Charleston. It stopped raining there, and the hole continued enlarging until the sun shone through from a perfectly clear blue sky.

The weather remained almost perfect over about a hundred square miles of the Kanawha Valley for the two days while we conducted our operations, though it continued to rain all around. Within an hour of completing our fieldwork, the sky clouded over and it began to rain again!

Other famous psychics (Peter Hurkos, Andrija Puharich, Joseph DeLouise, Ingo Swann, etc.) have visited the area and reported unusual "amplications" of their talents.

Try this some time. It is a great game. All you have to do is lie in a deck chair on a sunny day with, preferably, puffy, fairly well-spaced cumulus clouds. Pick one of notable shape that all of you agree you can identify; then shut up and concentrate on it in whatever way you feel best.

It is really quite alarming how your particular cloud appears either to dissolve within minutes, or to behave in a strange manner, like changing color or turning into a wisp.

Mind you, we are not suggesting that this is a practicality; rather, that it is a fine demonstration of "psychokinesis," and to a reasonably high power.

What might cause a cloud to crackle, fizz, or pop is of great Fortean import.

We do hope that some of you will be able to dig out some previously published and documented cases of noisy clouds, or let us hear of any personal experiences you may have had with them.

CHAPTER 5

EARLY EUROAMERICANS – APRIL 1969

In *The New York Times* of Sunday, October 20th, 1968, there appeared a brief but very pertinent article by our member, Andrew E. Rothovius (Member No. 100), who is also secretary of that most excellent Society, the New England Antiquities Research Association (NEARA) of New Hampshire.

The article was entitled "Mystery Hill's Riddle: 1600s or 3000 B.C.?" It describes present work at a site of that name near North Salem, New Hampshire, which has puzzled scholars and laymen alike for several decades.

The site comprises a number of small but massive structures with tunnels, drains, what appears to be an altar slab, and other curious features that could possibly be interpreted in different ways – as either a colonial cider-press, a maple-syrup refining plant, a potato processor, etc.

The history of the place is very garbled and obscure; there are records of its having been much larger in colonial times, with masses of other constructions having been vandalized for their stones. Many other nearby sites are of similar odd construction.

The really interesting paragraph in this article is, however, and we quote:

> At the 33rd Annual Meeting of the Society for American Archaeology, Robert A. Kennedy of the Pembrokeshire County Museum, Wales, reported that a "substantial body of sound archaeological evidence can be presented to demonstrate that such early trans-Atlantic contacts actually took place between 3500 and 2000 B.C. The pottery evidence alone is irrefutable."

This would seem at last to bring us face to face with not only pre-Columbian, but also pre-Erikson infiltration of the Americas from the east.

It has always seemed strange to us that the general consensus of opinion, both popular and even scholarly, should be that nobody "discovered" America prior to the Norse; when, at the same time, everybody has accepted the fact that the Amerinds came from east Asia across the Bering Strait, and the Eskimos later, by the same route.

The very idea that an endless stream of Korean, Japanese, and Chinese ships, sometimes with survivors aboard, could have drifted around the north Pacific via the Kuro Siwo and east wind-drift currents, has always put everybody into a tizzy; but that Europeans could have deliberately boated over here – when still in what is termed a Neolithic stage of civilization, invariably produced much more dire repercussions.

Now, however, facts are beginning to make themselves felt, and an increasing number of scholars on both sides of the Pacific and the Atlantic are, one by one, taking quite a different view of the matter.

NEARA, for all its youthfulness, has played not a small part in this, since they and their members have been plowing through, investigating, mapping, and describing a seemingly endless list of Neolithic stone structures scattered all over both North and South America.

The result has been that many old myths (such as that claiming the Northern Amerinds "did not build in stone") have fallen by the wayside, while a host of other alternatives have come to light.

First went the Columbus myth, then the Norse, the Phoenicians, and finally, the copper and early Bronze Age folk with their hill-forts, bison corrals, megalithic graves, and other monuments.

We've had Phoenician inscriptions – in both of their scripts, and even with the names of certain of their kings on both – from the Amazon since the 1870s; now we have Bronze Age (of Europe) type pottery in the northern hemisphere of the U.S.

The Phoenicians in South America constitute a matter that we will have to take up at greater length later, but let us just quote from the excellent publication, *The Log*, Vol. II, No. 6, of June 1968. On page 103, the news editor reports:

> Prof. Cyrus Gordon of Brandeis University thinks a tablet he has translated proves that Phoenicians touched the New World 2000 years before Columbus.
>
> An inscription on the tablet, left by a crew of 12 men and 3 women, tells how their ship left the Gulf of Aqaba in the company of nine other ships, during the reign of a sixth-century-B.C. king of Sidon, named Hiram.
>
> Dr. Gordon feels the ship was blown off course, on a trip around Africa, before 500 B.C., and ended up on the shores of Brazil. The tablet bearing an inscription was first discovered in Brazil in 1872.

Shades of poor Professor Ramos in Brazil?

[Editor's note: Professor Alcita Rita Ramos was a widely known defender of the civil rights of indigenous Brazilians, particularly the Yanomani tribe, and is author of "Indigenism: Ethnic Politics in Brazil," among other books.]

CHAPTER 6

ANCIENT EGYPTIAN ELECTRICIANS – JULY 1969

A most disturbing new concept is arising to plague us. Concrete evidence of this is coming in at an increasing rate, and Forteans are just going to have to shift another gear, and fast, because for once we show signs of being overridden both by the mystics and the scientists. Yet, if anything was strictly down, or up, our alley, it is this. The reasons for our having overlooked or deliberately ignored this development are, we believe, twofold.

First, Fort died before the dawn of the modern technological age, so that those who took him as their starting point for their general interests were not confronted with it. Second, we feel that honest Forteans have been scared away from it, due to its having for a long time been a particular pet of the mystics, religionists, and armies of kooks and crackpots, including promoters of lost continents like Mu and Atlantis.

The matter at issue is whether there was a worldwide technological civilization on this earth in extremely ancient times, and certainly before 4000 B.C.

The concept of ETs – or "ETIs" (extraterrestrial intelligences) as some are now calling them (even by such people as the scientists who worked on the benighted Condon Committee) – having visiting this planet throughout our historical period, and before we evolved some two million years ago, and even to the very start of our Earth as a cosmic entity, is now quite acceptable.

Even Dr. Carl Sagan, who is more or less the father of exobiology, suggested just this as a possibility in his book, *Intelligent Life In The Universe*. The researches of Charles Hapgood (Member No. 7) into the origin of ancient maps (see his *Maps Of The Ancient Sea Kings*) seem to prove (as nearly as anything can be proved) that some intelligences mapped the whole surface of the earth circa 20,000 B.C., using most refined trigonometry, and probably did so, for the most part, from the air.

But the idea of mere humans running around laying coaxial cables, using computers, and building batteries circa 4000 B.C., just about when agriculture, writing, astronomy, and other simpler things are believed to have been "invented," is asking perhaps a little too much of pragmatists. But there is now very concrete evidence of such advanced technology, so that one is forced to ask the question: How?

There are dozens of suggestions but, as we see it, there is only one (as of our current state of knowledge) that is outstanding; this is that not only the basic enterprises like agriculture, medicine, writing, religion, law, and so forth, but also a full-blown technology were brought to this planet, at the same time, and possibly by the same entities.

The best bet is that this took place just about 20,000 B.C., and that said entities first mapped the joint, then landed and started getting our evolved ancestors organized by herding them into "Gardens of Eden" and so forth, and "teaching" a priesthood to govern them, by exercise of a limited knowledge of practical technology.

Then they buzzed off again to look for more water planets. This they would appear to have done about 5000 B.C., either leaving us wholly on our own, or under the care of a few supervisors and home-trained priests.

According to this notion, being virtually thrown on our own resources for the first time, we proceeded to make a monumental muck-up of everything, as is apparently our specialty. The trouble may have been that then, just as now, we simply had not been sufficiently educated to cope even with the basics, let alone the residue of advanced technology.

This latter was left in the hands of the priesthoods, but they rapidly went mystical and forgot how to make and run the essential machines, though some hung on for millennia and did not completely lose their minds. A few of the basic things did take hold, like metallurgy; and it was this that, more than anything else, kept the remnants of the pre-ancient, ET technology glimmering.

A most puzzling and provocative example of a possible residue of higher ET technology is a certain hieroglyphic from Egypt, from Hall 5 of the Temple of Dendera, showing what looks like a modern lightbulb.

Nothing like this has been found elsewhere in Egypt. Each figure appears to be bearing an object of very carefully composed form, which would seem to be transparent, since items that look like snakes are shown within. These transparent constructions seem to be inserted into solid bases with some kind of circular, perhaps threaded, closure at the end.

From each of these come what look like coaxial cables, which join and run into a little altar. Each main structure is apparently supported on a pedestal. There are those who have contended that these are an elaborate form of the sacred symbol known as the ankh, but frankly, they look much more like certain modern insulation fixtures for very high tension power lines. The large transparent objects look like enormous "lightbulbs" containing heavy filaments.

Naturally, any Egyptologist who is asked to interpret this depiction will come up with a wild explanation, simply because one just cannot have priest-technicians wandering around in Egypt four thousand years ago, installing high-tension cables with what one engineer suggested were some very clever "male" and "female" (i.e., positive and negative) terminals.

Meantime, however, Barney Nashold (Member No. 87) rolled in from Chicago. He and his wife have been on a SITU expedition to Central America during the past year. When we showed him this frustrating business of the Egyptian "whatever-they-ares," he really flipped, because he has, over the years, accumulated a file of drawings taken from Nazcan and other South American painted ceramics, which appear, on detailed analysis, to be formalized (and in part "allegorical") layouts for electronic circuitry.

Ivan Troenig's *Kulturer Fore Istide* ("Culture Before the Ice Age"), published by Nyloms, Uppsala, Sweden, in 1964 describes the Dendera devices as high-tension dischargers. Member Number 15 and his esteemed cohorts made this assessment:

> Certain elements, especially the cables, are virtually an exact copy of engineering illustrations currently in use. The cable is shown as very heavy and striated, indicating a bundle of many (multipurpose) conductors, rather than a single high-voltage cable.
>
> As a matter of fact, a high-voltage cable would be much thinner; if the insulation were required to be that heavy for extreme high voltages, or moderately high voltages at high currents, rest assured that no technician would be holding the associated device. Corona leakage would get him most swiftly. The supporting stands would have to be much taller and heavier to withstand such voltages.
>
> It is much more likely that the cable is, as stated, a multi-conductor, wrapped and insulated with an outer jacket. If this were a lightbulb, the maximum size of both would be explainable by heavy current demands; but mega-voltage insulators of such large size would not be required.

> It would seem to follow that moderately high voltages are in use. A connector is obviously employed; some type of supporting base to glass seal seems apparent. However, the two bulbs are not identical, as shown by the designs on their sides, and the base stands. I do not think that they are transparent, as the technician's body is not visible through the device; it would seem more obvious that these are identifying markings, or codings (as a type number on a TV camera tube); probably indicating correct usage of the device.
>
> Since the cables seem to originate at the altar, one wonders if this is a manually controlled setup, or remotely controlled. Further, with both devices set at an angle, and shown aimed at the wall, could they not be the ancient equivalent of the modern TV projection system?
>
> One should also note that the two "technicians," especially the one on the left, seem to be wearing a mask device (eyeshield?); and unless the drawing is badly reproduced, both have some type of apparatus in their ears, suggesting the equivalent of modern TV cameramen, complete with radio receiver and/or earphones for direct instruction during a "show."

Engineers are wonderful, especially when they contemplate matters outside their strict regimen. There was a rider to the above from this fraternity that stated: "It should be noted in passing that the priesthood(s) of old were past masters at 'putting on a show' to impress the local natives. And what could be more convincing of their 'magical' abilities than a mysteriously appearing (and disappearing) image on a temple wall? After all, the best way to impress the natives is to scare them half to death."

The replies so far received from the archaeologists and historians, and notably Egyptologists, have been in marked contrast to these pragmatic comments.

Several to whom we applied have not even answered; one said he could not translate the hieroglyphs shown in the depiction, and another said he would not! When it came to the business of trying to identify this Temple of Dendera, we ran into some pretty obvious chicanery.

Everybody seems to transliterate Ancient Egyptian names in their own ways; we have Denduras, Dendaras, Dhenduras, and on and on, but the most popular form of our temple among these savants seems to be the little one-room temple of Dendur, which has now been acquired by the Metropolitan Museum of New York, and which is being re-erected under a special dome in New York's Central Park.

This temple of Dendur has no such depiction in it, naturally.

So devious have been the responses of the Egyptologists that we have applied directly to the government of Egypt. So once again, we must ask you to wait.

How many more centuries, one can never tell.

CHAPTER 7

AN OPEN LETTER TO ALL UFOLOGISTS – OCTOBER 1969

Since the publication of the Condon Committee's report, and the book *UFOs? Yes!* by Dr. David R. Saunders and R. Roger Harkins, we have received a mounting flood of requests from radio and TV talk programs throughout the nation and Canada for interviews with our members on the current status of ufology.

We have handled dozens of requests directly from our headquarters since February, and we have referred twice as many to interested members outside the northeastern area. In addition, there have been many long-distance "beeper" interviews, the exact number of which we cannot keep track of, as they crisscross the continent.

As a considerable percentage of these interviews have been on the larger network shows and leading local programs, we have hit a very large and wide audience.

The response as analyzed from mail and reports from program producers is exceedingly interesting because it falls, almost to the letter, into two clearly opposed camps. The composition of these has come as a considerable shock to a lot of people, though it was not altogether unexpected by us.

It transpires, in fact, that there is a clearcut break, and even antagonism between, the ET buffs (from old-guard ufologists to the wildest saucerians) and the general public. The former are almost a hundred percent infuriated with our stance in this matter; the latter are literally ebullient in their agreement with our attitude.

We believe that we have stumbled across the explanation of this seeming paradox. Once again, it seems to be basically a matter of semantics but, in this case, bolstered by a simple lack of knowledge of the facts.

In the case of the general public, this is due to a lack of real information on the subject, augmented by the flood of misinformation that has been poured out by officialdom, "sciencedom," the press, and the buffs themselves. Even those who have not been specifically interested have become sickened with this folderol, and so have given a prolonged and concerted cheer at being given the opportunity to listen to a little common sense.

The ET buffs, on the other hand (most notably those who set themselves up as being "scientific" in their procedure and approach), appear, one and all, to be hooked on some particular pet theme; not to have any training in true scientific methodology; and not to have acquainted themselves with the facts as published.

And this is where the matter of semantics comes in; a visiting member pointed out to us that the buffs everywhere could not tolerate our approach to it. The reason? That we are "so diffuse." Upon enquiring what this might mean, we learned that most buffs are not interested in the overall picture of their specialty, or its "how" and "why."

Further, they believe that science should be concerned only with the collection of data (i.e., the "what"), which alone they call "fact." This is exceedingly interesting and probably true. Moreover, it might explain why not only the buffs, but also those scientists who have taken a serious interest in ufology, have got precisely nowhere.

Data collection is a pleasant pastime, and the essential primary basis for scientific investigation, but it should not be an end in itself. In a subject such as ufology, moreover, if it is pursued to the exclusion of speculation, hypothesis, and theory, it is often worthless.

Even if you analyze, by computer, rooms full of "reports" on funny lights and other things in the sky, what have you got? Maybe evidence of temporal or spatial incidence, shape, color, behavior (alleged), and suchlike, but the whole exercise is useless unless you have at least some theory as to how such statistics should or might be interpreted.

None of the buffs have any real theories, except some of the older organizations that insist all UFOs are machines (but deny that they could contain living entities, we should note!), and the "contactees," who seem convinced that they are all manifestations of glorious "space people."

No wonder our opinions do not find favor with any of them.

We therefore suggest to the buffs that they might profitably read the books that we recommend, since the opinions expressed in these are going to continue to be offered to the general public through the mass media, and on a massive scale, by us.

Further, these opinions are open to discussion and criticism by everybody, including scientists, technologists, ufologists, saucerians, and all other interested parties, both private and public.

Those wishing to indulge such debate had better do their homework, however, and get their facts straight, before criticizing those whose works we have recommended. This is something the buffs have persistently refused to attempt, but the general public has apparently made a valiant effort to attempt – an effort that has so far, unfortunately for them, proved futile and frustrating.

CHAPTER 8

IN PURSUIT OF THE ADDENDA – JANUARY 1970

There are a few items of general interest; the first is the matter of what are called poltergeist manifestations. What causes these purely physical and measurable "manifestations" would seem to fall into the category of lifeforms (i.e., biological), since they seem to be entities, and possibly to have an intellect if not a mind.

That they may be invisible (invisible to some but not to others), or able to become visible, is beside the point. It is what "they" do that is of interest to Forteans, since these doings are perfectly tangible. Thus, one discusses such doings as expressions of the behavior of some lifeform.

The second item is the matter of brain control or "mind patrol." A living entity at the evolutionary state of mankind is manifestly composed of four interlocked and coordinated units. These are a purely physical body; a computer built upon biological principles and run by electrochemical mechanics, and which we call a brain; a mind, or intelligence, or intellect that is completely intangible, but which can be probed by such mentalogical procedures as psychology; and finally, a personality, which may be called a soul, spirit, Id, or what-have-you.

It now transpires that we, by taking thought upon the matter, can, to a considerable extent, control the physical body. During the last quarter century, we have made giant strides in controlling the brain. Such outfits as the Brain Research Institute of UCLA, in Los Angeles, have no less than fourteen thousand cooperating scientists, with doctorates, throughout the world.

Much has also been done – but little published – on the rather unpleasant matter of mind control, or control of the intellect.

This is an overly sensitive area of research, smacking of Orwell's "1984." But when it comes to tampering with the individual personality of a living entity, it appears that, at least so far, we are completely buffaloed.

Maybe one day we will find out how to influence or even alter the basic Id of an individual but, as of now, it appears that the only way we can do this is to eliminate or "erase" the entity (or original personality) and start all over again.

But then, there is still the greatest of all unexplaineds: the UFO. Here we run into something that does truly stand outside all the rest. We must first accept that these entities exist. Given this, we have to take note of the fact that, as of now, they display both tangible and intangible qualities.

They are, in fact, as we have said several times before, basically cosmic, in that they represent a whole "other world," or represent another spacetime continuum, or universe(s) – however you choose to define it. Whether they are machines, lifeforms, or robots, they present us with aspects of all segments of our wheel of knowledge. They may be infinitely varied in origin, construction, and intent, but until we have gotten at least one and tried to analyze it, we have no starting point for asking questions.

COUNTING DRACULAS

A delicious story appeared in *The National Observer*, of the 8th of December last year, written by Nancy A. Palmisciano of Boston College.

This was titled: "Dracula Lived, Say Two Professors, And He Was a Cruel Romanian Prince." This report goes, in part, as follows:

> Since Dracula was written in 1897, the classic horror tale about a diabolic vampire has been raising goose bumps on millions of youngsters and adults. But was Count Dracula pure fantasy? Could he have existed like such infamous characters as Hungary's Countess Bathori, who had 650 girls murdered in the 17th Century?
>
> Radu Florescu and Raymond McNally, two Boston College history professors, often discussed such a possibility. The two professors were particularly intrigued by Stoker's exacting biographical information on Count Dracula. The descriptions of Transylvania and historical references astonished Prof. Florescu, a native of Romania and an expert on Balkan history.

Slowly the pieces fit together. Dracula emerged as Vlad Tepes ("Tepes" means "the impaler"), a Romanian prince who ruled in Walachia from 1456 to 1462, and again in 1476, before he was assassinated. Official diplomatic reports of the time also refer to him as Dracula, a name he may have derived from his father, Vlad Drakul, or "devil."

Professor Florescu isn't sure how the vampire myths grew about Dracula, but the bats that lived in the castle may have played a part: "There are records of bats, which may have been rabid, flying from the castle and attacking and biting people in the area. To the peasants, the deaths that followed must have seemed to be the work of a demon."

One pertinent fact here is that the Central American Indians told the first Spanish arrivals that they knew horses very well, but that all of theirs had, only a short time before, been exterminated by bats. Another pertinent fact is that certain bats, like the Desmodus of Asia, carry rabies and several other diseases undesirable to both humans and livestock. They regularly bite fruit and insect-eating bats that share the same caves and hollow trees, and thus transfer diseases to them.

Note then that rabies, like syphilis and other diseases, turned up in a new and particularly virulent form in Europe just about the time "Columbus sailed the ocean blue." Further, rabies comes in two forms, called technically "furious" and "paralytic." These usually alternate between carnivorous (like the Desmodus) and herbivorous or omnivorous animals that they bite.

Most human victims develop the paralytic form, but sometimes they become "furious."

We have always contended that so-called vampires may have been humans infected with the negribodies of rabies, but who developed this furious form and went around biting people and animals, and lapping up their fresh blood.

SEXUAL ATTRACTANTS

In our issue of April 1969, we noted the matter of the effects of bathing on the destruction of natural epidermal exudates (i.e., body odors due to soaps and other unnatural products).

Some ten years previously, we had stumbled across some scientific reports (made by medical investigators in Munich, Germany) that impinged upon this question, but which were designed to explore a related matter; namely, the part played by the various and numerous natural exudates of the animal body, in this case including saliva, those ejected along with the sperm by males, and the complex of female vaginal fluids.

Body fluids were taken from both male and female volunteers, sterilized, and then incorporated in candies. These candies were then distributed, at random, to young but mature people, both by the original donors and by other unknowing volunteers.

Careful and detailed records showed that within very brief periods, an inexplicable number of the recipients had paired off, somehow found each other (often over very considerable distances), and were in bed together for the natural purpose of copulation.

No single participant ever could offer an explanation as to just why he or she so behaved.

The conclusion of the experimenters was that reproduction is stimulated by copulation, but that the latter is not the same as the former (although the same physical organs are used for both). This theory had been put forward twenty years before, by Davenport in England, as a result of his studies of sex in chickens.

The theory is basically that reproduction is actually subsidiary to copulation, per se, and in a manner of speaking, nothing more than "a convenience" to the natural process of the continuity of the species.

The act of copulation, on the other hand, is much more vital, and specifically to the individual, in that, apart from kissing, it is just about the only way by which body fluids may be transferred directly between individuals.

Said fluids – quite apart from the ova and spermatozoa – constitute enormously potent complexes of powerful enzymes and other chemical triggers for metabolism, growth, and so forth. The male absorbs as much from the female during proper prolonged copulation as does the female from the male – hence, among other things, the reason for the histological composition and construction of the prepuce in mammals.

Copulation would, however, be random and highly adventitious without some method of selection and attraction, and this is provided by the body odors of animals, including our species. There can hardly be any argument about this in view of the work of the father-and-son team of Maastricht, Holland, the Olischlagers, the greatest rat killers of all time, who achieved their phenomenal success by tracking down, chemically, the substances exuded by rats that attract the opposite sex.

Using this, they brought the rats to poisoned bait, something that those clever creatures had previously learned to avoid in very short order. As a result, sexual attractants have now been developed for a wide variety of vermin and furbearing animals that are trapped; and these substances may be bought in stores specializing in hunting equipment. In other words, animals cannot resist body odors.

A final observation on all this must be that the most expensive French perfumes can never be a substitute for what nature built into its sexual attractants, and this would now seem to be borne out by Professor John Law's findings:

> John H. Law, Professor of Biochemistry at the University of Chicago's Pritzker School of Medicine, bases this hypothesis on the fact that insects and animals often communicate sexual attraction, as well as alarm or the discovery of food, by means of body odors.
>
> Law is conducting research on pheromones – organic compounds excreted by animals as a form of communication. "Olfactory communication," he says, "is probably one of the oldest and, in some cases, the most efficient means of communication employed by animals."
>
> Among humans, this form of communication may have existed, but was dulled by the evolution of verbal language and civilization: "What the human race may be missing is suggested by the fact that if a woman's perfume was as potent as the pheromone used by the female silkworm moth to attract the male of the species, and if a man's nose were as sensitive as a moth's antennae, one drop would stagger men blocks away."

CHAPTER 9

LITTLE GOLD AIRPLANES A THOUSAND YEARS OLD – APRIL 1970

This fascinating item got lost in the shuffle, due to its having been asked for as an article by *Argosy* magazine. At the risk of being heavily censured by that publication's editors, we are constrained to observe that the article they produced was lousy; and for the following reasons...

First, the photos reproduced did not display the essential points: second, those that they did publish were not only irrelevant, but misleading; third, not one of the photos or drawings mentioned in the text were reproduced.

We now have to add to this the fact that a great deal more has been learned about these items since the publication of that article, and no less than a half-dozen more little gold pieces, of identical or very similar design, have turned up all over the place – notably in the Chicago Natural History Museum and in the Smithsonian Institution.

The whole business has, as a result, become greatly more important.

If you look at photographs of the original item from the Columbian National Collection, as found for us by Mannie Staub (Member No. 117), and of the Chicago specimen, you will note the differences in the outlines of the wings, as seen from above, which would seem to put the latter into a different class. However, when seen from the side, the two are identical, but for the design or "lettering" on their upright tailfins.

This "other class" is comprised of two-dozen more items of similar size, and in several collections, which appear to display a progressive development from, and/or deterioration of, the original models, which are fairly simple and straightforward. These become ever more elaborately ornamented and fantastic.

The most interesting point here is, however, that they do not become more naturalistic as they should if later artists and artisans, working from early planelike models, had tried to convert them into the form of known animals they knew so well and modeled so precisely. To the contrary, they become ever more fantastic, showing, we tend to believe, that they knew the original things from which they made their models were not animals, but inanimate things that we would call "out of this world."

It is interesting to note also that the article mentioned above hardly caused a ripple among the reading public. This puzzled many at first, but then it was pointed out that the age of these artifacts had hardly been mentioned, and certainly not stressed.

There came then a rather startling discovery. This may sound obnoxious to many when stated flatly, but it is simply that a very high percentage of the public today, and notably the younger generations, labor under the most extraordinary delusions about history. For instance, the notion that Henry Ford invented the automobile is almost universal, just as is the belief that Edison invented the electric light, and that just about every other currently used technological development (TV, radar, radiotelescopes, etc.), were first invented in the U.S.

But more alarming is the discovery made recently that youngsters, brought up on misinformation techniques as everyday facts of their lives, have absolutely no concept of historical background.

As a result of this appalling ignorance (which is not their fault, but that of our so-called educational system and TV), the idea that some South American Amerindian artists were making little gold models of swept-wing jet planes a thousand years ago means nothing to them. The general attitude, we personally discovered, was a sort of "So what?" This was often followed up with, "What's so great about that?"

The "discovery" of these little artifacts is probably one of the most pertinent ever made through archaeological enterprise – if it is a true discovery – and it has become much more pertinent since more of these items have come to light, and aerodynamics engineers and designers have had a chance to analyze them.

The original notion that they were "zoomorphic fantasies," which was nothing more than a desperate resort on the part of archaeologists and historians faced with such an alarming mystery, has now been completely demolished by the zoologists who, with all the will in the world, simply cannot come up with any animal that has the features of these items; meanwhile, so many of those features are exactly and precisely those of airplanes.

At least a possibility has therefore to be faced; namely, that somebody had airplanes circa 500 to 800 A.D. in northwestern South America, and that local artists made models of them to the best of their ability.

The question as to who made the things that formed the models for these little pendants, presents quite another problem. There are three alternatives: either there was a highly developed human civilization thereabouts at that time (or earlier); these things came out of the sea, and were devices built by some underwater civilization; or, they came down from the sky (perhaps from outer space), and were subsidiary craft employed by intelligent entities from elsewhere, who are engaged in visiting, surveying, or colonizing this planet.

CHAPTER 10

CHAOS AND CONFUSION: OLD SAWS OF FORTEANA – JULY 1970

Our purpose, as good Forteans, is to present all matters of a tangible nature that have not as yet been adequately explained; but, at the same time, to do all we can to find adequate explanations for them.

The oddities and paradoxes that keep cropping up in the established fields of scientific enquiry (and which now follow this column) are every bit as enigmatic as these intellectually chaotic items that are handled herein. It's just that being asked to cope with the oddities first is asking an awful lot of those who do not have the time to keep up with the abstruser findings of "orthodox" science.

This is an old saw, but coming from a dentist we have to take note. It ties in with a couple of other things that cry out for confirmation and elucidation. But first, the story:

> Daytona Beach, Florida, 9th April 1970: A housewife who has been receiving musical radio signals through her teeth has a mouthful of new fillings today, but still may be driven to extraction.
>
> The woman, who agreed to talk about it only if her name wasn't used, said Wednesday she had all her fillings (but one) replaced by plastic. She said a metal filling was left, because it involved a root and might have to be pulled.
>
> The music stopped for three days. She had been picking up the signals since the night of March 16, and had been sleeping in a motel, out of range of her neighborhood, to get peace. "I thought I was free, and was ready to throw a party," she said.
>
> Then her teeth tuned up again, much weaker than before, but still there.
>
> Electronics experts say they believe the music is being transmitted by a person using a wireless phonograph to send signals to another part of his house. A dentist, Dr. J.H. Long, explained that two metals such as gold and amalgam fillings, plus acid in saliva, could set up a potential receiving system, such as the woman's mouth.

> The housewife placed an advertisement in a newspaper urging whoever had been playing the songs she was hearing to identify himself. The numbers include *Long Way to Tipperary* and *Rambling Rose*, she said. She said the ad brought a flood of calls, "but nothing concrete."

Our first question is: why only music? The experts may be right in that the lady was picking up a hi-fi radio or intercom. However, similar reports have been coming in since the initiation of regular broadcast programs in the early 1920s.

Many of these stories were suppressed, because the sufferers heard voices as well, which they interpreted as "evil spirits" haunting them; and who, as a result of being unable to obtain relief from psychiatrists, were toted off to mental institutions. We wonder just how many well-adjusted unfortunates have been so toted off, only to end up truly insane.

It is, of course, just possible that the ultraterrestrial intelligences can, and do, pester good people with dreary music and a running commentary of a frightening or obscene nature. This would seem to be their wont and pleasure. However, there is another lead-in to this phenomenon.

Way back in 1916, a Mr. James McKelvie, who was a partner and confidant of Marconi (he used his steam yacht, the *Surf*, in conjunction with Marconi's *SS Electra*, to first skip the Atlantic Ocean with radio relays), was staying in a hotel at Tintagel, in Cornwall, England. He complained that the springs in his bed were picking up Morse-coded signals; and, being one of the leading experts in the diffusion of such at that time, he started keeping a record in shorthand.

Through his position, which was semi-official, he was able to trace the messages to certain British naval craft, operating within a limited range of Tintagel; and he then proceeded to somewhat upset officialdom by forwarding to them samples of these ultrasecret, encoded Morse-code communications.

Electronic engineers take an extremely dim view of the suggestion that two different metals used as fillings in teeth, bathed in buccal acid saliva, can act as radio receptors; and they take an only slightly less dim view of this bedspring bit, which has likewise persisted, year after year.

THAT UFO ATTITUDE

In this column in our last issue, we endeavored to explain our attitude to this business. Being pragmatists, we did not expect everybody to understand what we were trying to say, but at least we said it! We will not reiterate, except to say, once again, that we are not in the least interested in "funny lights in the sky."

On the other hand, we are deeply interested in any reports – however wild – of touch-downs, alleged landings, or what are now called "occupants" of seeming machines or other objects that appear to be material, and which appear to come down from the sky or up from waters (sightings over bodies of water are, believe it or not, twice as prevalent).

In other words, like the gallant Dr. Condon, we are open to the reception of any reports, but preferentially to those that are other than mere unidentified lights in the sky. The reason for this is as follows.

After years of active involvement in this curious business, we have become persuaded to a number of concepts or, as Charles Fort called them, "acceptances." These were completely contrary to the persuasions of others who got into this field only after WWII.

Starting in 1948, we found, somewhat to our amazement, that the enthusiasts, almost to a man, were stuck with the notion that all these things were 1) of extraterrestrial origin, 2) machines or constructions, which for some extraordinary reason, 3) could not have occupants!

In no case did we ever hear, in the U.S. or Canada, any of a number of much wider implications and more basic questions, which had been asked about this phenomenon, for centuries, in the Old World and in Latin America.

The mere mention of such concepts was enough to provoke howls of derision from all parties vaguely interested in the matter, including officialdom and sciencedom, and, most curiously, the mystics.

The first of these concepts, and the most ancient, was that unidentified and unexplained objects seen in the sky were of wildly multiple form, and displayed a bewildering variability of behavioral patterns.

Second, just about the only feature all UFOs tend to display, was their ability to appear and disappear at any speed (up to the ultimate, meaning instantaneity – in turn, of course, meaning an ability to teleport).

Third, whether there be intelligent life with corporeal bodies, or other gross bodies, in our universe or not – i.e., we being unique in this respect – the possibility of the existence of intelligent non-corporeal bodies has, for centuries, been taken under advisement.

Fourth, nobody except the North American saucerians and ufologists ever, for a moment, questioned the possibility, if not the reality, of the existence of other universes, or, in Einsteinian phraseology, "space-time continua."

Every religion, including even science and communism, has always contended that there is an interrelationship between our continuum and at least one other, if not with many others. The Gautama Buddha reached the conclusion long ago: we are in touch with, and influenced by, an infinity of other existences.

All of this, and the millennia of thought that had gone into it in the Old World, even apparently among the indigenes of Central and South America (and, it seems, among our North American Amerinds), was either totally unknown to this new breed, calling themselves "ufologists," or was deliberately ignored by them.

At the same time, their ignorance of the findings of modern, "western," pragmatic, mechanistic science was not just abysmal, but virtually total. You don't have to be an Oriental to conceive of infinity, though it does come hard to a westerner; but without this capability, you will never be able to understand the ultimate findings of even our own pragmatic science.

How can one expect ufologists to grasp the significance of parapsychics, in view of this ignorance – an almost pathological denial of anything they have not previously accepted?

Most curious of all is the fact that it has been those whom we call, and usually rather scathingly, the "mystics" who have come closest to reality, though their interpretations have always been, and still are, all "wet." But they cannot be blamed, because they lacked, until very recently, the ultimate and most essential tool – namely, pragmatic physical science.

In the immutable progression of discovery and understanding, this tool comes last. Imagination comes first, then belief, then theorizing; but the whole exercise is worthless if you cannot test your theories. This is actually all that science does.

In the case of UFOs, pragmatic scientists have run into a block that – if they are technological scientists – they cannot overcome. However, if they are philosopher scientists, this hurdle becomes merely a challenge.

What has happened to "ufology" is that it has reached a point where our presently accepted technology has balked. If we are going to probe further into the mystery, our materialistic technology will have to be expanded into fields presently unimagined.

CHAPTER 11

FABLES OF THE UFO AGE – AUGUST 1970

How about ascertaining UFO facts rather than attempting to prove or disprove the fantasies generated in 23 years of controversy?

Flying saucer news and information has been heavily censored for the past 20 years – not by the government, but by the two dozen or so researcher-writers who have been most vocal on the subject. Of these, only a small handful have tiny fragments of information, many of which are irrelevant to the overall picture.

And to make matters worse, investigative methods of the UFO buffs have been designed to cope with the criticisms of the skeptics rather than making any sincere attempt to set the complex and contradictory UFO data before the public. The rest, more often than not, have seized upon the extraterrestrial conclusion, and then carefully selected those reports that appear to fit this conclusion.

They have "brainwashed" you by busily discarding everything that fails to conform to their speculations, and by carefully tailoring their "evidence" to fit their conclusions. Astounding fantasies have been founded during their attempts to study the phenomena.

There surely is no question that some sort of unknown phenomenon does exist. All kinds of UFOs were seen, reported, and documented by the military services during World War II. The Air Force always has admitted that a certain number of cases could not be explained; the Air Force never has denied the existence of the phenomenon, but has claimed that a certain percentage of all sightings could be explained as natural phenomena, misinterpretation, etc., and that no scientific evidence has been uncovered to support the claims of the UFO buffs.

Now let's stop the fun and games, and examine some of the neglected facts and facets of the UFO situation, and compare these facts with the speculations of the buffs. For our purpose, a "fact" is based upon identical observations in several different parts of the world. Thus, if six teenagers report a bizarre incident in Nebraska, and an identical incident is reported from South America and/or Australia, and is repeated in Canada and/or Norway, we can assume that this phenomenon has basis in fact.

The reliability of the witnesses becomes less important than the incident correlations! And it is time to compare some correlated facts with the popular speculations of the UFO buffs.

For instance… It is a fact that throughout history, strange, unnatural substances have fallen from the skies. Slag (industrial refuse) fell on Darmstadt, Germany, in 1846; slag reportedly fell from a UFO over Puget Sound in 1947. Many other substances reportedly have fallen from UFOs over the years, and in nearly every case, these substances have proven to be ordinary earthly materials such as aluminum, magnesium, silicon, etc. There are hundreds of these cases from every country on Earth.

But because buff fable insists the UFOs are of extraterrestrial origin, any physical substance falling from them must consist of alloys unknown to earth. Therefore, all of these cases are hoaxes!

But if the ET buffs had systematically collected all of these fragments instead of discarding them, and made the necessary correlations, they now would have an impressive body of evidence proving that UFOs do exist, and are manufactured from, or utilize, common earthly materials.

It is a fact that it has been frequently and reliably reported that the unidentified objects have executed sharp right-angle turns while traveling at high speed, thereby defying the known laws of inertia. (Any occupants caught in such a maneuver should be crushed by "G," or gravity forces.)

But Buff Fable insists that such maneuvers prove the objects are the product of an "advanced technology," and as such must come from another planet.

Nevertheless, such maneuvers indicate only that the objects operate outside the known physical laws. They prove nothing of the object's origin or technology.

It is a fact that the objects frequently have been reported to travel at incredibly high speeds within our atmosphere (they have exceeded 25,000 mph on radar). Yet they produce no sonic boom. Any physical object traveling at such speeds would have to displace air and produce booms.

Buff fable has it that the absence of sonic booms indicates, again, that an advanced technology is involved.

Actually, the absence of sonic booms indicates that the objects are either nonphysical (mirages, projections, etc.) or are composed of substances of less density than the air around them. In other words, these objects may pass between the molecules of air rather than force these molecules aside. Again, this points to something outside our known physical laws, but not necessarily outside our planet.

It is a fact that in many documented cases, the unidentified objects have landed in snow or mud without leaving any marks, and UFO occupants have been observed under similar conditions, and they too have left no footprints behind. (There are now hundreds of such cases.)

The UFO buffs automatically reject these cases as "hoaxes" because of the absence of physical "proof."

It is probable that both the craft and occupants in these cases are nonphysical in our sense of the term. They could be of a different density. They reportedly have been seen to leap or "fly" long distances and jump easily over high obstructions. Because of a density difference they may, therefore, be unaffected by gravity in the same way we are.

(The irony here is that the buffery accepts the absence of sonic booms as proof that the objects are extraterrestrial, but the absence of ground markings or footprints is regarded as proof that the sighting report is erroneous or a hoax.)

It is a fact that numerous witnesses have reported UFO occupants walking through the seemingly solid walls of grounded saucers. There is also a growing list of cases in which witnesses have claimed that occupants walked through the walls of homes, into the faces of solid hills and cliffs, etc.

The buffs generally reject these reports outright, and they rarely are published in the buffery journals.

Nevertheless, these incidents lend additional support to the thesis that some of the objects and their occupants are nonphysical and of a different density, enabling them to pass through solid matter in the same way that smoke passes through a window screen.

It is a fact that in the early 1950s, one Colonel Maitland, USAF, inadvertently flew his jet fighter straight into *and through* a large UFO he was pursuing.

The buffery shelved this report, and it hasn't been mentioned since. But obviously Colonel Maitland's UFO was of a different density than his airplane, because the two were able to occupy the same space at the same time.

It also is a fact that over 50 percent of reported sightings involve objects described as being transparent or translucent.

The buffery tends to shelve such reports and concentrate only on sightings of apparently solid objects.

But while the buffs have tried to convince everyone the objects are solid machines, over 50 percent of the sightings suggest that they are not solid. And perhaps they are not machines!

Another fact: in a large percentage of cases, objects viewed at low level visibly change their size and/or shape while in full view.

Buff fable ignores these cases. Nevertheless, this surprising nonphysical characteristic further suggests that many of the objects are not machines.

It is a fact that in hundreds of landing reports, the objects are said to have appeared or disappeared instantly. In such cases, the objects often appear suddenly on the ground. Then instead of taking off they vanish – often in a bright explosive flash.

The few UFO buffs who have studied these cases have assumed that the objects simply took off so fast they couldn't be seen.

There are two other "impossible" answers: the objects can become invisible either by becoming totally transparent or by bending light rays around themselves; or such objects are three-dimensional projections (like a laser hologram) and do not physically exist.

Ivan Sanderson and others suggest still a third possibility — that the objects move from place to place by teleportation or instant transference.

It is a fact that thousands of reports from the 19th and 20th centuries describe unidentified objects that suddenly exploded in midair and disappeared. Some of the Scandinavian reports in 1946 also mentioned this peculiar characteristic.

Buff fable insists the objects explode when caught in a radar beam. But this hardly explains the cases from the 1800s, or the innumerable radar sightings in which the objects did not explode.

In actuality, no one has bothered to collect and study these intriguing and possibly significant cases. Since those exploding UFOs usually are audible, the noises may be caused by air rushing in to occupy the space where a material object had been. In some cases, the exploding object apparently sprayed fragments over the area, but no fragments could be found. In the few cases where such fragments have been located, they proved to be aluminum or magnesium. This kind of data deserves extensive study.

It is fact that in a majority of all UFO reports, both historical and contemporary, only flying lights were observed; no solid object was visible.

Buff fable says a solid object is hidden within these lights, and the illumination is caused by ionization of the air produced by the theoretical electrical field surrounding the craft.

As a matter of fact, many of these lights are only a few inches in diameter; yet they behave in a controlled, intelligent manner. While some of these lights may be part of a larger, unseen craft, many of them probably are nonphysical, and might be similar to what we call "focused radar."

Another fact in evidence: the solid, definitely configured disc or cigar-shaped objects with windows, fins, antennae, and apparently metallic construction are quite rare in comparison to the type of reports outlined above. They constitute a minority of the total sightings.

But buff fable has concentrated on these sightings, thus basing its speculations on only a small fragment of the data available.

Actually, since the solid, machine-like objects are the rarest of all, they may represent the least important of the overall phenomenon. A really significant study of the UFO mystery must include a study of all the reported phenomena — not a superficial choosing of those cases that seem to support a single theory.

What with overlooking or ignoring a large proportion of the available data, it is little wonder we are failing to comprehend or explain UFOs. Clearly, a large part of the phenomena suggests nonphysical characteristics beyond the grasp of our present-day science.

We've had our eyes shut for a long time, yet the UFOs haven't gone away. It's time to find and try a new approach.

CHAPTER 12

INTRODUCING "FAFROTSKIES" – OCTOBER 1970

One simply cannot keep writing out in full: "Things that fall from the sky," so we are using a new acronym: "fafrotskies."

"Branding" is a matter that has been going on throughout the ages, and which formed the real core of Charles Fort's efforts throughout his life. Despite the acceptance of the reality of meteorites a century ago, and of unreliable manmade devices orbiting the earth a little over a decade ago, the endless rain of things from above has neither been explained nor explained away – probably because no one came up with a name for the falling objects.

The number and variety of these fafrotskies is entirely unknown to the general run of citizens, and not even fully appreciated by the most dedicated Fortean. The matter appears, however, to have become of increasing concern to officialdom, even if "sciencedom" positively refuses to have anything to do with it.

As an example, we quote from a letter from our esteemed Member No. 459:

> I enclose an article from a local paper, about a fafrotsky, which may interest you. The metal that fell, when cracked open, is like well-polished silver, but is much harder. About 10 years ago, two similar pieces fell at the same time in this town. All missed houses by narrow margins. An authority on meteorites came here from Buffalo, New York, 120 miles away. He said that for certain it was not a meteorite.
>
> NASA heard about it. They sent in a detachment of armed soldiers and demanded the two pieces, which were in the possession of two women. One refused to give hers up, but her attorney told her she must. She outsmarted them and kept a piece that was 20 inches in diameter.
>
> *Reader's Digest* offered her $2,000 for the story, but soon withdrew without explanation. She phoned the management and asked why. He said they had orders from the government not to publish the story. What nonsense is this?

The newspaper report is from *The Potter Enterprise*, of Coudersport,

Pennsylvania, dated August 19th, 1970, and goes as follows:

> Philip Lehman, son of Mr. and Mrs. Luther Lehman, Sweden Valley, has a knack for finding things and Friday night, August 3, was no exception. While watching television in the James home in Sweden Valley, Phil caught a glimpse of a mysterious glowing in the sky. Upon closer investigation, he watched a sparkling thing fall to earth.
>
> Phil and his friends ran to investigate, and found what appeared to be a large rock lodged in a hole, probably created from the impact of its hitting Earth. Phil tried to pick it up, but the shiny object was too hot to touch. Pieces of cardboard were used to remove the rock from its resting place. A strong kerosene odor was noted. Later, a sample of dirt from the hole was taken, and this strong odor still lingered.
>
> The mysterious object is heavy for its size, weighing over ten pounds, while having a diameter of only five inches. Density, calculated by Mr. Lehman, is 7.12. Physical characteristics include silver and gold coloration with patches of blue. Its surface is pitted and rough, and yet there are no sharp edges. The Lehmans had difficulty in chopping pieces of the rock, to send to officials in Buffalo for analysis, and the chipped place reveals an inner surface silver coloration.
>
> An interesting sidelight to the story is a similar rock found 10 years ago, almost to the day, by the Donald Kelsey family near their camp, two miles from the Lehman sighting. The Kelsey rock was similar to the new object, and upon analysis, was believed to be a piece of titanium nitride. NASA officials took the rock for analysis, and it was never returned.

There are several Fortean aspects to this report. First, we have things falling in the same limited area over a considerable time; the Coudersport paper states that a Mr. Carl Smith found a similar odd stone 25 years ago, long before the dawn of the age of Sputniks.

Second, we have a categorical statement that this item is not a meteorite. Third, comes this endless refrain of military personnel descending upon the area and impounding the fafrotsky. Such allegations are almost standard for anything connected with a UFO, but much rarer when it comes to seemingly simple, straightforward accounts of "meteorites."

The introduction of such cloak-and-dagger is really very odd, as is the note that the lady's attorney advised her to comply with the request by the military. This statement comes from a private individual; but when a newspaper boldly states that NASA basically filched a specimen, we begin to wonder.

For the edification of the ET buffs and all those others who delight in the shadow world of James Bond, we should perhaps put some facts on record. In 1967, a treaty was signed by the U.S., providing for the rescue of astronauts and the return of equipment, including "space junk," to the country of origin. The U.S. and the Soviet Union have implemented this agreement several times.

Further, a legal subcommittee of the UN Committee on the Peaceful Uses of Outer Space has been working for over six years on a further treaty covering liability and compensation. Thus it is incumbent upon our government to do everything it can to get there fastest when anything is reported falling from the sky, and to obtain it for analysis.

The only pity is that these facts are not publicized and made known to the finders of these falls, in officially printed form. Such a procedure would allay a lot of fears, stop a lot of wild speculation, enhance the position of the government, and encourage cooperation, resulting in greatly enhanced reportage.

The average citizen would doubtless be only too willing to help in this rather grizzly operation, especially if it were pointed out to them that the better our cooperation with the Soviet and other governments with space programs, the more likely we are to get back not only our own junk, but also our *astronauts* if they land in foreign territory.

Nonetheless, we must not let this be given as an excuse for all fafrotskies. Manufactured items were falling centuries before Sputnik I, and it is manifest that tons of live frogs or fresh blood do not originate from any manmade space probes.

FOOTPRINTS ON THE BLOOM

This is an extremely sticky one. It has been building up for years. It is quite "balmy," yet we feel it is about time that it be dragged out into the open. So, "let the chips fall where they may." Airing this business is not going to do anybody any good; but what use are we, if we do not at least stick our necks out?

As of now, this business requires a full-length book treatment, but this would take a couple of years of further research. Therefore, we feel it incumbent upon us to put on record, for your edification, the outline of the facts as known to us now. This will doubtless not be believed by anybody, but we give what references and documentation we have available, and you can then take it from there.

That which we are talking about is the appearance, or alleged appearance, of the imprints of various things, in the form of either individual footprints or of tracks of such imprints, in solid rock, that look as if they could have been made only by live things; but which, according to our current understanding of the chronology of the deposition of sedimentary strata, should not have existed when those rocks were laid down.

It is rather startling to make a list of such reports that have been issued over the past century. They crop up in old scientific journals, in the records of historical societies, in popular science magazines, outdoor magazines, municipal courts, and in local newspapers (though very much less often in this medium than one might expect).

Said reports range from those of imprints that look exactly like those of dinosaurs – but in strata that are either far too old or too young, by millions of years – to miles of completely inexplicable tracks in rocks dated way before the earliest known to contain any fossils, namely, the Pre-Cambrian.

For the moment we will concentrate on reports of human-type footprints. This is where the seemingly "balmy" aspect of all this comes in – at least, it should seem as such for anyone who has ever read anything of what is known about geochronology and/or paleontology. So, to the facts as published:

1. *Silliman's American Journal of Science*, Vol. V (1822), pp. 223-231; and Vol. XLIII (1842), pp. 1842. Prints of human feet were found in "secondary limestone" along the Mississippi between New Harmony and St. Louis, later identified as limestone of Mississippian-Lower Carboniferous age.

2. *The American Anthropologist*, Vol. IX (1896), p. 66. The perfect imprint of a human foot, 14-1/2 inches long, was found 4 miles north of Parkersburg on the West Virginia side of the Ohio River, in a large stone (stratum unknown).

3. *The Field*, ca. 1948. An imprint, apparently of a shoe, found near Lake Windermere, England, in what is believed to be Ordovician limestone.

4. *The Seattle Post Intelligencer*, 15 April 1963. A footprint measuring 44 x 21 inches (wait a minute!) was found in sandstone at Baxter Springs, Kansas. The print is that of a right foot, the toes are perfect, and there is a deep indentation produced by the ball of the foot (stratum unknown).

5. *The Dallas Morning News*, 7 September 1968; and 16 and 29 August 1969. In the limestone bed of the Paluxy River, near Glen Rose, Texas, there are "manlike" footprints, up to 21.2 inches long, in the same stratum with dinosaur tracks.

6. Letter, dated 12 September 1969, from Dr. Wilbur G. Burroughs, formerly Prof. of Geology at Berea College, Kentucky, now retired. Dr. Burroughs discovered human-like fossil tracks in a nearly horizontal bedding plane of massive gray sandstone (Pottsville, Pennsylvanian System), in Rockcastle County, Kentucky. They averaged 9-1/2 inches in length.

7. *The Trenton Times*, 14 July 1968; *Fate*, December 1968. Fossilized sandal prints were found at Antelope Springs, near Delta, Utah, in Cambrian limestone. One print had embedded in it a squashed Trilobite. (Massive reports and correspondence on file at SITU.)

8. A color photograph of a tiny footprint (i.e., shoeprint) 1-1/4" long, in opalized rock, from an opal mine in northern Nevada. This could be of any date, geologically, in view of the establishment now of the possibility of almost instant petrifaction. But how come the size?

Assuming that those who have not been interested in matters geological might miss some essential points about all this, we put on record that, while the most primitive man-creature's remains have now been dated as some 1-1/2 million years old, paleontologists now rather confidently believe that there were no mammals of any kind, nor dinosaurs, or even any reptiles, when these Mississippian and Pennsylvanian strata were laid down in what is called the Carboniferous Period – the age of which is given on the new chronology as between 340 and 250 millions of years ago!

That was the first reason why we say this whole thing is "balmy." The second point that should perhaps be stressed – though we admittedly wonder why any such admonition should be necessary – is that three of these cases (the very ones for which we have authenticated photographs) are not of naked human footprints, but of sandals or shoes with heels!

The idea that there were bipedal primates, with feet like ours, running around 300 million years ago is mad enough, but that said hominoids wore shoes, with very carefully designed heels, would appear to put the whole matter utterly beyond the pale; and, particularly, if it is noted that in the case of Antelope Springs, said imprints have been most thoroughly analyzed and appraised by a shoe designer and manufacturer.

A third point that one supposes should be made, is that these imprints, and more so the tracks, were not discovered on top of, or outside slabs of sedimentary strata or non-sedimentary boulders. These human-type imprints, with shoes, came to light when rocks were being quarried, and they were found on the surfaces of laminae (layers) "inside" stratified deposits – and, in some cases, dozens of feet below the present surface, and hundreds of yards back into the quarries.

Thus, quite apart from the enormous ages of the strata themselves, we are confronted with the secondary enigma of these imprints somehow having gotten into these profoundly subterranean situations. If these are deliberate hoaxes (as many will surely say), chiseled out of the rock by funsters, then how was it done! How did the funsters get them into solid rock a hundred feet down, and a hundred feet in from a quarry face, and then arrange for some fellow to split the right two laminae apart – in the presence of witnesses – to disclose the hilarious fake?

Come on, skeptics; can't you do better than that?

The only more obvious answer to all this is that these imprints were left by some bipedal, motile, presumably living entities who (or which) wore foot protections such as we call shoes, and who were wandering about this planet 300 million years ago.

Since we have no evidence that any such living entities had been evolved on our planet at that time, and since we have a lot of evidence that they had not, one can but presume that these sandaled or booted folk came here from elsewhere.

Take it away, skeptics.

CHAPTER 13

THE DEATHRAY AT LAST, OR HOW TO TURN OFF RIOTS IN ONE EASY LESSON – JANUARY 1971

As reported in *The London Sunday Times* by Frank Dorsey:

> A team of French scientists in Marseilles is working on a deathray machine designed to provide an entirely novel method of human destruction. The project began when the electro-acoustical laboratory of the French National Center for Scientific Research moved into a new building three years ago. The staff complained of headaches and nausea.
>
> Investigations began. Electromagnetic waves were suspected, and all stray ones detected were eliminated; so also were all ultrasound waves, which have been the laboratory's major interest for 18 years.
>
> One of the technicians got out an antique apparatus for detecting *infrasound* – that is, air vibrations that oscillate at less than 10 vibrations a second, or 10 Hertz. (The human ear registers, as sound, vibrations from 16 per second, or 16 Hertz, to 20,000 Hertz.) It quickly identified the source of the unease: a giant ventilator in a factory next door.
>
> Sound is a succession of waves in which the air is alternately compressed and decompressed. Fast vibrations either go right through solid objects or bounce off them, usually doing relatively little harm even when very powerful. But slow air vibrations, below the hearing level, can create a sort of pendulum action, a reverberation in solid objects that quickly builds up to intolerable intensity.
>
> The wavelengths most dangerous to life lie below seven per second. At this point, one has a vague impression of sound and a feeling of general discomfort. At 3.5 Hertz, nothing can be heard directly, but there is a curious incidental effect. Nearby sounds, such as air hissing into a pipe, take on a pulsing quality. All sounds in the neighborhood seem to ululate rhythmically.
>
> The research team has suffered from its experiments. Some of

> the invisible injuries appear to be persistent. These infrawaves not only affect the ears, but work directly on the internal organs, causing a rubbing together of various adjacent organs because of a sort of resonance. This provokes an irritation so intense that for hours afterwards, any low-pitched sound seems to echo through one's body.
>
> To study this phenomenon, the scientists built a giant whistle hooked to a compressed air hose. However, when turned on, the "test nearly cost us all our lives," said Prof. Vladimir Gavreau, who is in charge of the Electro-Acoustical Laboratory. "Luckily, we were able to turn it off fast."
>
> He went on. "All of us were sick for hours. Everything in us was vibrating: stomach, heart, lungs. All the people in the other laboratories were sick, too. They were very angry with us," he ended laconically.

After this, they kept the power input very low, and started probing downwards from the 16 Hertz point, and came upon the critical point of 7 Hertz at which, if used in a huge whistle as much as 18 feet across, with a small airplane engine to rev the fan, they estimate that people could be killed, en masse, up to five miles away.

One would have thought that we already have enough ways of killing off people, but it must be admitted that, if you want to do so, this would seem to be a perfectly splendid way of doing it. In warfare, it would be a lot neater than using nerve gases and/or bacteria, and probably more "humane," if you gave the enemy the full works in one blast.

But it would seem that the best use for such a device would be for controlling or eliminating mobs during riots. You could soften them up with a bit of nausea and disorientation, and if the idiots persisted in continuing to riot, you could lay them out for a day or two, thus avoiding the necessity for a massacre, which always seems to upset people.

WERE EGYPTIANS FIRST IN AUSTRALIA?

This was the headline on a short piece from *The London Sunday Express*, sent us by Member No. 162. It was datelined Sydney, and read as follows:

> Did Ancient Egyptians surf at Bondi, a suburb of Sydney? Historian Rex Gilroy plans to lead an expedition into central

> Australia to prove that Egyptians and other races found Australia thousands of years before Captain Cook. He believes he already has evidence that Arab dhows explored the New South Wales coast about 3,500 B.C.
>
> He is studying a collection of bronze plates, coins, pottery, and hieroglyphics found near Bondi and in other parts of Australia. Now he will search for huge reliefs of Egyptian deities, reported to have been found by Aboriginals on a cliff face in central Australia.
>
> "These discoveries could rewrite the history of Australia," said Mr. Gilroy, director of the Mount York Natural History Museum. "Evidence of the landings of Egyptians, including Aboriginal carvings of their dhows and clothing, is coming to light all the time."

This is intriguing, though one wonders which "Arabs" they mean. Had Mr. Gilroy said Phoenicians, it would seem more likely. Also, the Egyptians were not notoriously good sailors, despite Thor Heyerdahl's latest success. Bear in mind that his *Ra* boats were built not by Egyptians, but by imported Bolivian Indians! Nevertheless, we pursued Mr. Gilroy.

Our own reference works having failed us, we called the Australian News and Information Bureau. They had heard nothing of it, and were no more successful in finding a town called Mount York than we had been; nor were they able to find any reference to Mr. Rex Gilroy.

We then wrote to the Foreign Editor of the Sunday Express, who very kindly checked with his correspondent in Sydney and sent us an address for Mr. Gilroy. In the meantime, we had also written to the Australian Museum in Sydney to ask their help. And we got it, in the form of one of the most refreshingly frank letters we have seen:

> I have your letter of 14th September 1970, addressed to the Director of the Australian Museum. Dr. Talbot, our Director, is at present overseas, but in his absence, I think I can completely answer the request made in your letter about Mr. Rex Gilroy, self-styled Director of the Mount York Natural History Museum.
>
> Without being too strong, I think I can state that you can completely disregard any claims as to discoveries, either of a natural history nature or archaeological, made by Mr. Gilroy.

> We have already notified all the responsible newspapers in Australia that they should disregard any claims he makes. His work is bogus, and he is possibly slightly deranged.
>
> He has a small private museum situated on the Blue Mountains of New South Wales near Mount York, (nearest large town: Katoomba). We have had trouble with him in connection with fossils – his claim that he has found traces of Arabs and Egyptians, in Australia, on many occasions.
>
> He makes wild statements to small local newssheets, which publish them as "sensational findings," and then these get extracted into large city dailies in Australian states.
>
> If you want some details as to his craziness, I would suggest that you communicate with our Curator of Paleontology, Dr. Alex Ritchie. I repeat, you can completely disregard any claims of Gilroy in this matter.
>
> Yours faithfully,
>
> Elizabeth Pope, Acting Director

It would be rather fun to have Egyptians and Arabs in Australia, but it seems clear that Mr. Gilroy has a bee in his bonnet. We would like to know more about the alleged "bronze plates, coins, pottery, and hieroglyphics" mentioned. We had actually written to him before receiving Miss Pope's reply to our enquiry. But Mr. Gilroy has not answered.

There are some very curious – and fully authenticated – Aboriginal paintings of people who bear no resemblance to any Australian Aborigine; they don't resemble any Arab or Egyptian, either. And, despite the fact that we have a tendency to be very cautious in accepting flat statements by orthodox scientists, the comments on Gilroy's general reputation indicate that anything he offers should be fully backed with facts and artifacts.

RED-HAIRED PEOPLE-EATERS

Scores of redheaded mummies, averaging 6-1/2 to 7 feet tall, and thousands of artifacts have been taken from a smoke-coated, exceptionally dry cave some 22 miles southwest of Lovelock, Nevada. Paiute Indians living in Lovelock state matter-of-factly that these were cannibals who preyed on the Paiutes, and were eventually exterminated by them.

The last remnants of the cannibal tribe holed up in this cave and were suffocated by enormous fires built at the entrance. Annie Bill, 68, a Paiute and a lifelong resident of Lovelock, said, "All members of the tribe who were exterminated had red hair. I have some of their hair, which has been handed down from father to son. I have a dress that has been in our family a great many years, trimmed with this reddish hair. Old Paiutes always called the redheads 'Siwash Indians,' but many of my people really wondered if the redheads were Indians at all."

Her grandparents told her that their grandparents described the cannibals as having long faces and light skin "like white man." This may seem a rather remote source of information, but non-literate peoples often do transmit their tribal history from generation to generation with remarkable fidelity.

The anthropologists and archaeologists are rather rude about the story of cannibalism and red hair, claiming that the color of the hair was due to "age or chemical action." And Donald R. Tuohy, curator of anthropology at the Nevada State Museum, has announced, apparently with some heat, that the Paiute stories are "myths – pure and simple fabrications."

He further "believes" that the Paiutes knew of the existence of the cave and its contents long before its discovery by white men in 1912, and concocted this story to explain it.

He is quite right on one count.

Sarah Winnemucca Hopkins, daughter of the Paiute chief, Old Winnemucca, published a book entitled *Life Among the Piutes* in 1883, in which she gives the whole story, and states that the last of the cannibals were exterminated by her people earlier in the 19th century. Recent carbon-14 dating tests indicate that the cave was occupied as late as 1800-1850, which certainly supports her story; and no one has even tried to suggest that this late occupation was by the Paiutes, who were never cave dwellers.

The question of who these cannibals were, and where they came from, is still unresolved. The earliest occupation of the cave is dated as somewhere between 2000 and 3000 B.C., but it was not occupied continuously up to 1800.

Most of the artifacts are what one would expect: baskets, nets, duck decoys, arrowheads, and the like. But one is most unusual. Preserved at Stoker's Museum in Winnemucca, this is a calendar stone marked with 52 dots on the inside, and 365 on the outside.

Clarence (Pike) Stoker, curator (and presumably owner) of the museum, has speculated that if the redheads weren't Amerinds, "It's very possible they were descendants of Egyptians who sailed to America hundreds of years ago." Red hair suggests Phoenicians rather than Egyptians. And Phoenicians do seem to have gotten around; but that they were all giants and indulged in cannibalism is questionable.

Current studies of the artifacts, mummies, and some 5000 human coprolites (fossilized excrement) may provide an answer to this conundrum. In the meantime, we think it impolite to call the Paiutes liars, and unwise to lean too heavily on Thor Heyerdahl's Egyptian exercises.

"THEY ALL DISCOVERED AMERICA"

The most startling pronouncement in the field of archaeology last year was undoubtedly Professor Cyrus H. Gordon's considered pronouncement that some Mediterranean people, probably including at least some Hebrews, got to this continent 1000 or more years before Columbus.

Dr. Gordon stated for the record that a tribal group of indigenes called the Melungeons offer clear evidence of this fact, not only in their legends, but also in their physical appearance. An inscribed stone was unearthed from one of their burial mounds in Tennessee, in 1885, by one Cyrus Thomas, who was working with the Smithsonian. He further stated that "this group of people are neither Amerindian nor Negro, and are Caucasian, but not Anglo-Saxon."

The stone was found under one of nine skeletons in the mound. "The archaeological circumstances of the discovery," Dr. Gordon said, "rule out any chance of fraud or forgery, and the inscription attests to a migration of Jews." It was brought to his attention by Dr. Joseph D. Mahan, Jr. of Columbus, Georgia's Museum of Arts and Crafts.

It has been lying in the Smithsonian since its discovery, but ignored because the inscription was initially read upside down and made no sense. It bears eleven characters (including five letters which Dr. Gordon reads as "For the Land of Judah"), in a style of writing used in Canaan around the beginning of this millennium, and he suggests that they were inscribed about the time when "Jews migrated here to escape the long hand [arm] of Rome after the disastrous Jewish defeats in 70 to 135 A.D."

He adds that the Melungeons are descendants of Mediterranean people, who themselves believe that they came to the New World in ships about 2000 years ago.

This is but another nail in the coffin of the "Ocean Blue in 1492" and all that "discovery" nonsense, and a cornerstone in the ever-growing edifice of Near Eastern exploration of, and settlement in, the New World, starting 2000 years before Columbus. It was Dr. Gordon, moreover, who jolted us, two years ago, by pronouncing another inscribed stone slab found in the Amazon basin as being of Phoenician origin.

Before that, we have the massive work of Professor Ramos, bringing to light dozens of other petroglyphs, including perfect fish and Indian rhinoceroses filled with Aramaic-type Phoenician letters. Add to these coins found in the bottoms of wells all down the eastern coastal plain of North America, tombs in South America, and statuettes of bearded men with Caucasian features in Central America, and the Columbus buffs begin to look a bit silly.

Sure, that splendid Genoese made it over, but he was accused of being unable to read the maps by his own captains! Don't you wish you had a map when "discovering" a new place? It would save a lot of time, trouble, and expense.

A point of interest may be worthy of addition to this matter. It is not generally realized that not all the Hebrew tribes of old were landlubbers. Several groups broke away from the God Yahwe and followed Baal of the Phoenicians (and the Palestinian coastal strip), and became sea people like the Philistines, and the subjects of the ancient sea kings.

They nonetheless remain Hebrews (the term "Jew" is a religious designation), and they were still around at the time of Columbus, usually as the specsioneers (or pursers) on ships of almost all nations, handling trading and financial matters.

There is the fascinating story of the specsioneer on Cortez' flagship, who was a Hebrew and who, upon seeing the first Ocellated Turkey birds, named them in Hebrew *tokhe',* since when they spread their tails, they displayed eyes on them, like those on peacocks' tails. (Incidentally, the turkey was first taken to Spain, but developed in Holland and Belgium, and then in the Spanish Low Countries. It did not spread to Turkey until very modern times!)

There is massive evidence that the crews of trading vessels from the eastern Mediterranean were always extremely mixed, and that not only the coastal Hebrews, but also the inland tribesmen did an awful lot of boating. Hebrews, and notably Sephardim, settled, in earliest times, at the terminals of sea-lanes everywhere. They were the brokers and the first maritime insurance agents. If the Phoenicians got to the New World, Hebrews undoubtedly arrived with them.

CHAPTER 14

UFOLOGY TRENDY? – JANUARY 1971

We are being asked ever more frequently why we appear to be decreasingly interested in this phenomenon. This does not mean that we have lost all interest in the subject; far from it.

The reasons for our current attitude are twofold. First, we are frankly bored with what are called mere "sightings" – a word which we abominate. They are endlessly repetitious, though we would be the first not only to admit, but also to point out, that no two are alike. In fact, we have a feeling that every damned one ever recorded is intrinsically different.

Nonetheless, recording the cases as of now serves only one purpose. This is to accumulate as much data as possible for the computerized analysis that is being undertaken by the Aerial Phenomena Research Organization (APRO) of Tucson.

We say this because we now believe it to be quite useless waiting for one of these things to "land" and be captured, or properly examined. If this could be accomplished, it would have been done long ago. Further, we have very good reason for thinking that it cannot be hoped for under present circumstances, and that it would not be comprehended if it were.

Let it be said that, while we say we are bored with "sighting" reports as a steady diet, we are increasingly keen to collect them, just as an entomologist collects up to tens of thousands of specimens of the same species of insect, because this is the only way by which one may classify variation; and by classifying variations, we almost invariably bring to light hitherto unknown and unsuspected facts.

But, for this kind of investigation, computers are essential, so we are shooting everything we receive on to APRO.

The second reason for our apparent indifference to this matter of late is quite different; and this is only an appearance, for it actually lies very near to the core of our own work and to SITU investigations. This may come as a bit of a shock to those of you whose primary interest is ufology, but it should be stated bluntly.

It is simply that, after very mature consideration, and an enormous amount of discussion and debate, we, as a body, feel that at least one sound, logical, and scientifically acceptable explanation of, and for, the phenomenon has now been offered; and, in view of this, we, as a scientifically based and oriented organization, feel that we should concentrate all our attention and energy on this theory, with a view either to producing worthwhile suggestions for those elaborating it to consider, or to collect measurable evidence of its invalidity.

This, in turn, should not be construed to mean that we are no longer interested in other theories. We most certainly welcome any and all, however crazy they may appear, because we have now entered the second stage of the old fundamental "What-How-Why" procedure. To reiterate: we now have enough "whats" to analyze, and should therefore proceed to examine all the possible "hows."

So far there is only one theory that has come to our attention that meets all the very stringent strictures that we place upon any and every theory. As far as we know, this was first mooted by Luis Schonherr in four articles in *Flying Saucer Review* of London, dated March-April 1963; January-February 1964; November-December 1965; and November-December 1968.

We say "mooted" because Mr. Schonherr actually speculated upon only one aspect of this concept: the physical one. This suggestion does not, however, appear to have been considered up to the present, though it forms a cornerstone of what we call (for convenience and easy reference only), the "New Theory."

This has now been put forward by more than half a dozen advanced scientists, several technologists, and four or five workers in other fields, notably journalism. Each has come to the same point independently. This we consider to be of the utmost significance, considering the standing of the scientists involved.

The new theory can be very simply stated, but the mechanics of it are enormously complicated and fairly advanced. It is based on established and proven – at least mathematically – theories, and form the basis of quantum physics. We have arranged for one of our members (No. 208), a nuclear physicist, to write up these technicalities for our next issue. For now, let it be stated as follows:

> UFOs, and several other types of "items," may be projections from another, or other, spacetime-continua that may be said – for simplicity's sake – to exist and to run on parallel lines to the one that we are in. (Of course, the word "parallel" is an oversimplification and, if taken literally, very misleading.)

This is an old theory, actually, but the current approach to it is novel, in that these projections are now being conceived of as holograms in form, but material in content. In other words, they "come through" from other dimensions, or "spacetime gravities," and go back into them; and can do so at any speed up to, and possibly surpassing, that of light. In other words, they are teleports.

Teleportation, meaning instant transference, is a term devised to cover the "transference" of solid matter through solid matter. Now, it would appear that this is a phenomenon that is fairly widespread. It is by no means infrequent in nature. But then again, as those who have propounded this new theory suggest, it now looks very much as if it can also be contrived artificially, even purely mechanically.

Thus, the theory envisages other continua (or other universes – a multiverse) inhabited by intelligent entities that have mastered the technique of artificial teleportation, and employ it to come through into our continuum, by what we may call "projection," and then influence our environment and us.

Further, these scientists consider that any such intelligences must have concurrently mastered the art of "creating" anything they want, ranging from UFOs to Little Green Men. And surely, if their chemi-physicists can make the former, their biochemists should be able to manufacture the latter. We are on the brink of doing both ourselves, after only about a century of serious consideration of the possibilities.

Until we do so, however, we will neither be able to capture, nor truly contact, either of them; for, from our present way of thinking, they are neither here nor there. They are both material *and* nonmaterial. They are, in fact, manifestations of Charles Fort's concept of Determinism Indeterminism.

CHAPTER 15

UFOOLOGY? – APRIL 1971

In accordance with our expressed policy, we once again have nothing of a factual nature to offer in this department. However, we do have something to say of – we believe – a practical nature. It is practicality that we feel may be of most use to the UFO enquiry.

Reports of observations of unexplaineds and inexplicables of a ufological nature are pouring into amateur, scientific, and official centers, and onto newspaper desks, from all over the U.S. and the world.

However, the general public is bored to death with the whole subject, and officialdom is apparently only too delighted that matters remain this way. Nonetheless, this does not mean that those interested in this natural phenomenon should abandon their efforts to further investigate it.

As we have said before, the best and most constructive thing that all of us can now do is help to assemble this massive overall compendium of what has been said and reported on and about this troublesome matter. Unless there really is some monumental hanky-panky going on, we still, after half a century, have nothing concrete to show for – but reports.

The very mass of reports itself is worth proper scientific recording, analysis, and enquiry; and the best way to do this is inputting the data into computers, so that we can have something to work with. With proper programming power, we could rule out whether the whole phenomenon is nothing but a monumental slice of baloney. We will never know if we never try, so please forward your reports to APRO for their database.

People interested in this business (of UFOs) fall into four classes:

1. The "Saucerians," who state that they have found a mystical, out-of-this-world connotation involved.
2. The sincere ET buffs who have been designated "ufologists."
3. The publicists, newsmen, and hack writers who make money out of the business, either deliberately or unwittingly.
4. A small body of professional scientists who are truly interested in the matter as a (natural) phenomenon, and who sincerely believe that there is something in all of it that demands proper

scientific investigation.

Only classes two and four are outright dedicated to a statistical endeavor such as APRO has set up. The other two parties are variously disinterested or actually averse to any such hardboiled approach to the subject. This is unfortunate, as both might contribute a lot to an ultimate solution.

The really sad aspect of this whole business is the "back-biting." There are a lot of very intelligent and well-informed people interested in this matter, and all of them are, personally, rather exceptionally charming individuals; yet, we are sorry to have to relate, we cannot, as of this time, name any two who agree on anything connected with the business!

Presumably they are all roaring individualists, but do they all have to demand that their ideas be the only valid ones?

Scientific enquiry, like any other, must proceed by argument and debate, but personal dogma must be relegated to its proper place, so that open debate can be maintained. The esoteric nature of this field does not mean it should be a haven for unprofessionalism. Misunderstandings due to standard exigencies of publishing should be kept to a minimum, so as not to depress the psyches of sincere laborers in this field.

(No one should be "jealous" of APRO. Can't we all grow up and cooperate?)

Let us make it quite clear that we at SITU are doing everything that we can to cooperate in APRO's data collection process, and we ask only that our members do likewise. A computer analysis of the material will further a true scientific investigation of the problem.

JUST PLAIN CHAOS: CAVEAT EMPTOR IN THE "BERMUDA TRIANGLE"

With the publication of Ivan Sanderson's *Invisible Residents*, a considerable amount of latent interest has been brought to light on the subject of underwater UFOs. The initial impetus for this interest came from a phenomenon to which the catchy title "The Bermuda Triangle" has been applied.

This is an area off the southeastern coast of North America, in which an excessively large number of ships, planes, and now some submarines have vanished – as opposed to simply foundering, ditching, or being wrecked.

Most newspapers – if they have not already foundered themselves, or been ditched or wrecked – can be trusted; they attempt to present only factual information, though "no one is perfect."

On the other hand, there are some weekly newspapers that deal in sensationalism and apparently do not hesitate to concoct stories at the drop of a hat. One such is a rag called *Midnight*, which published, in its March 22nd, 1971 issue a particularly irresponsible – even pernicious – article on the so-called "Bermuda Triangle."

This takes up the center spread, with a booming headline: "Government Physicist Discovers: UFO Base Off Florida Coast," and alleges that "flying saucers" are responsible for disappearances in the Bermuda Triangle.

Much of the article consists of quotations attributed to a Dr. Jonathon Wright, of whom it is said: "Dr. Wright heads a special-priority UFO investigative department at NASA. He also participated in the UFO study carried out for the Air Force at the University of Colorado two years ago."

Because of the allegation that NASA has interested itself in UFOs, we determined to track down "Dr. Wright." Our first step was to check the Condon Report: no Dr. Wright listed anywhere. So we called Dr. Thornton Page, who is now permanently attached to NASA. He had never heard of Jonathon Wright, and very generously stated that he was "going upstairs" to check all NASA directories. He would call us back.

He did: no Dr. Jonathon Wright. In fact, Dr. Page was so intrigued that he had also called Dr. Carl Sagan – who has never heard of him, either. Despite the cheery photograph of "Dr. Wright" included in the article, he may be a figment of someone's imagination.

And Dr. Page informs us, categorically, that NASA has no such department within its ranks, and wants nothing to do with UFOs. They are not interested in joining the "burnt fingers club" started by the Air Force.

Much of the rest of the material in the article is either puzzling (inaccurate) or pure drivel. For instance, it is stated that all disappearances in this "vile vortex" took place in December, which is rubbish. But what really disturbs us is the wholly unwarranted emphasis (fear mongering) on the idea that "I'm never going to fly across the Bermuda Triangle again, because I'll disappear."

It is perfectly true that planes and ships have vanished in the lozenge-shaped area off the southeastern coast of the U.S. It is equally true that thousands of people cross that same area safely every week!

Of course, it is dangerous to go to Bermuda: you may be hit by a truck on your way to the airport, your plane may crash on take-off or landing, or you may slip on your hotel steps and break a leg. Any one of these is far more likely than that you will disappear into thin air.

Admittedly, the possibility of a mere accident causes much less distress than outright disappearance, simply because an accident is considered a "normal hazard" that happens to everyone.

I suspect that if we began to say that when someone disappears into a vile vortex, he actually slips into another universe "where the land runs with milk and honey and there are no income taxes," we would soon see a definite upsurge in tourist traffic to vortices and "window" areas, vile or not.

It is, of course, the uncertainty that unnerves people. But no one gives up shopping for groceries because of the dangers of being hit by a car, despite the fact that far more people are disposed of in this way, every year, than have vanished into the Bermuda Triangle.

You want a vacation in Bermuda? Go ahead! The so-called "Bermuda Triangle" is not a triangle and has, so far as we can determine after considerable study, nothing to do with Bermuda!

Seriously though… After checking the allegations of such an exceptionally high incidence of disappearances therein, we initiated a critical survey of all Bermuda Triangle-type reports everywhere. The result was that there appeared to be ten such areas precisely distributed around the earth – five in the northern hemisphere, and all centered some 72-degrees apart longitudinally; and five others similarly apart in the southern hemisphere, but all shifted about 20 degrees to the east.

Next, the location of these ten anomalous areas was plotted, and at first, correlations were found only with surface ocean currents. However, both military and commercial pilots began supplying us with factual data of another nature. This was to the effect that in, or immediately around, these ten areas there appeared to be factual evidence of a time anomaly.

By this it is meant (to over-simplify) that a plane may appear to have arrived at its destination either much too soon or much too late, according to its instruments on the one hand, and by ground records on the other.

This "anomaly" is becoming apparently more frequent, and we therefore want to receive any and all reports of such incidents. However, please keep in mind that we are interested only in cases that are backed up with factual statistics or records.

We are also, of course, interested in receiving reports of ships or planes that vanish without trace anywhere – either new reports or old ones, since we certainly do not have a complete record of these.

Then, something else connected with this wretched business has cropped up. This came up after a Dick Cavett TV show broadcast, on ABC, on the 16th of March, on which our director (Sanderson) was to debate this whole business with Arthur Godfrey. On two previous occasions, Arthur had told Dick, and his audience, that he would be willing to do so but, in his good old style, referred to it as being "a lot of bloody nonsense."

Arthur Godfrey has been just about the loudest frontman for aviation during the thirty years he has been on radio and television, but he certainly slammed down the SST that evening, and everybody expected him to let the poor old "Bermuda Triangle" have it just as forcefully.

But to everybody's amazement, he not only treated the matter with the utmost conscientiousness and sympathy, but also gave three flat statements confirming this mystery from his own personal experiences. Also, at the end of the show, in reply to a query from Cavett as to whether he felt the matter warranted proper scientific investigation, he replied – directly into the camera – with a flat "yes."

The three cases that Arthur related on the air were demonstrated on a small globe we had provided, on which the ten known areas of anomaly were clearly marked. As he pointed to a spot in the Pacific on the globe, he spoke of the instant and complete disappearance of a great airplane, called simply "The Mars," northeast of the Hawaiian Islands.

Arthur told us that he was to have been on this flight, but missed it, and so watched its departure on radar. Snapping his fingers at the camera, he said: "The darned thing just went 'puff.' They never found a trace of it."

His second personal experience was when he was on his around-the-world flight in a twin-engined jet, and started to fly across the infamous "Devil's Sea" north of the Bonin Islands in the west Pacific. He told us that they lost radio and instrument contact for an hour and a half, and with only four hours of gas to go. Arthur stuck his finger on that blob on our globe and said simply: "And that's not nice, I'm telling you."

His third case was even less expected. Arthur asked for the globe again and, turning to Dick, he outlined the Bermuda blob and pointed out that the east coast of North America really curves way in. He told us that he and other experienced fliers en route from New York to Florida usually cut across the ocean, so saving a hundred miles or so, but that they had to keep an awfully wary eye on the instruments! (Pilot Robert Durant of SITU used almost the same words on Barry Farber's radio show.)

This information and confirmation given us by Arthur Godfrey set off a chain reaction among scientists and engineers. And it was one of the latter fraternity who came to us, the very next day, with an observation that has necessitated our dropping just about everything else. His suggestion: simply that the earth is a gigantic static-electric machine, having not just five dipoles – represented by the ten lozenges, "triangles," vortices, or whatever you want to call them, but six – the sixth pair represented by the north and south magnetic poles.

Immediately upon starting to work on this assumption, all sorts of extraordinary things came to light, and some very "old saws" cropped up. We are loath to bring one of these up, but it is none other than the old "hollow earth" business. This we will be reporting on later but, in the meantime, we beg that you do not suddenly think that our earth is hollow, or believe any other of the ravings of those who have suggested that it is. No: the matter at hand is a great deal subtler than that, and it stems from true and proper scientific theorizing.

CHAPTER 16

SERIOUS UFOLOGY – JULY 1971

We are extremely pleased to be able to report that one after another of the serious-minded ufological journals are beginning not only to publish listings of reports, but also to analyze them statistically. The British, French, and Spanish are hard at work, and we understand there are more such surveys upcoming from Denmark and Sweden.

At least three groups in the United States speak of eventual computerization when enough material has been assembled to sort out the factors to be analyzed. This is all very encouraging, but we are once again beginning to have doubts as to the efficacy of all this. More and more, it seems to look as if these phenomena come from other universes, as opposed to astronomical bodies in our visible universe. There could be reasons why this will make it impossible for us to identify them, even taxonomically.

First, as Einstein pointed out, there could be an infinity of other universes, so that there could be an infinite variety of UFOs, from which no amount of statistical analysis will produce anything tangible. Second, we have to contend with our New Theory, now supported by Jacques Vallee, which is that not only are we dealing here with intelligences immensely superior to ours (and technologies to go with these), but also that these creatures can create, spontaneously, anything they like, anywhere and any time.

Further, they themselves may have no corporeal existence, per se. They may be more like "minds," and thus invisible to us.

Now comes then the next question. Are what we call UFOs really solid and "real," according to our definition of reality, or are they like mirages that can be photographed? The electromagnetic effects that they cause are not incompatible with the second notion; likewise, thermal, chemical, radiational, and even sonic manifestations could be explicable.

And, speaking of mirages, most of them have not in any way been explained, notably those mediaeval-looking towns seen in the skies over Sweden, in which people could be clearly seen going about their business. And how about the Spanish fleet that sailed over the Sahara, which was filmed by a French film crew on location in Morocco? Many of the ships were later identified from their pennants, which jibed with sixteenth century naval records.

Might these not be other constructs of a nature similar to UFOs?

All of this speculation leads us directly to consider two more well-established phenomena: poltergeists and the so-called humanoids. They, too, could be mere constructs: the first invisible, the second visible to at least some of us. Cats, owls, and, as it now appears, many other predaceous animals, can see way out into the infrared spectrum, and so can hunt warm-blooded animals in total darkness.

Some of the smaller wildcats can also see some things that we cannot, even in bright artificial light. In fact, it begins to look as if our environment is perpetually loaded with all manner of entities. Some could be indigenous to this earth; others need not be.

Our technology is creeping up on these unseen worlds. Will we be allowed to take a look at them? Superior intelligences might well prefer not. But then again, if they have such ultimate power over us, what would they want with us in the first place?

Is it not possible that they have always been controlling our evolution, and educating us to a point at which we could be ready to take a peek at the greater reality? We have said before that there is nothing illogical in supposing that this planet is nothing more than a nursery, as Charles Fort constantly remarked.

About a month ago, as of the time of writing this, a Mr. Elliot Carlson, a staff writer for that august newspaper, *The Wall Street Journal*, rang us to ask the very simple question, "Whatever happened to flying saucers?"

Since this gentleman was a professional journalist, we attempted to answer his question, which we felt was realistic rather than purely rhetorical. It was really very simple; the only reason for supposing that the number of reports had dwindled away almost to zero, as most people seem to think, is that newspapers have given up printing them!

However, to back up this contention, we sent Mr. Carlson quite a lot of material, and references to the massive summaries being published in Canada, Australia, Sweden, Denmark, Britain, France, and Spain. Last week (June 14th), his story about UFOs appeared on the front page of his paper.

This is a typically fine piece of *Wall Street Journal* reporting. Unfortunately, however, Mr. Carlson didn't do his homework; but, rather, relied on the now moribund organization called NICAP (National Investigations Committee on Aerial Phenomena), which has never done its homework, nor the daily work for which it was set up to do (investigation).

It would seem that NICAP does not read other ufological publications – especially foreign ones. But then, has always been a little chauvinistic (in addition to being called "racist," at least by one former member). Furthermore, from one statement in Mr. Carlson's story, it would appear that NICAP has – for the *third* time in its sixteen years of life – decided to commit suicide. *The Wall Street Journal* stated it thusly:

> Then again, the buffs expect UFOs to be around for a long time – an outgrowth of a theory that asserts the existence of another universe located very close to Earth's.
>
> Only "it is invisible, because it's on another space-time continuum," explains Ivan Sanderson, director of the Society for the Investigation of the Unexplained.
>
> "However, beings from this other universe sometimes choose to appear here physically, which they can do by manipulating various timewarps."
>
> NICAP derides all this as bunk, but nonetheless refuses to accept the validity of the Condon Report's conclusions.

NICAP was founded by a professional promoter, on a somewhat grandiose scale and with a sensible-sounding prospectus, so that a number of prominent people accepted positions on its Board. Said promoter then set about to "murder" the enterprise, by turning it into a sort of intellectual circus. The thing would have foundered then and there, had not Major Donald Keyhoe come to the rescue, and managed to get this gentleman to resign.

Serious-minded ufologists were greatly encouraged, and the organization immediately assumed top place in the field – and internationally at that. However, their new approach to the subject almost immediately got into another rut. This was the adoption of a paradox as the basis of its policy: namely, that UFOs were/are machines, but that, at the same time, they did not, and could not, have occupants.

This turned off anybody with any scientific training for, while we indeed had robot machines as probes, such as we used before the manned lunar landings, there could be no possible reason for asserting that such machine-probes could not be manned. This ruling cut off any possibility of analyzing reports of said occupants – just as much as it did those of the so-called "contactees."

Then Don Keyhoe got into an argument with the U.S. Air Force, and for some years, NICAP's efforts seem to have been devoted almost exclusively to lambasting that already embattled outfit, thus antagonizing not only it, but also most other departments of government. The organization also got into one hell of a financial mess.

NICAP has loosened up a bit intellectually, to the extent of admitting the possibility of "occupants," but their heart doesn't seem to be into making such leaps. Not even *The Wall Street Journal* can save them from their grumpy infirmity.

TIME TRAVEL

The following fascinating little ditty comes to you fourth hand, but no doubt our members who subscribe to *The New Scientist*, *Science Journal*, or *The American Journal of Physics* can clear up any misunderstandings. The former carried a story that was too good to miss, in its issue of May 27th, 1971:

> I was my own grandpa in a tachyonic way.
>
> If tachyons, hypothetical particles that travel faster than the speed of light, really do exist, we had better start rethinking our concepts of time, free will, and history.
>
> According to L.S. Schulman, Indiana University, Bloomington, resolution of tachyon paradoxes about which comes first, the cause or the effect, can lead to a very static picture of history. Using physicists' parlance: "History is a set of world lines essentially frozen into space-time." (*The American Journal of Physics*, Vol. 39, p. 481)
>
> While we may feel strongly that our actions are determined by our past history, our present may also be a product of our future. Consequently, free will may be tossed out the window.
>
> Schulman cites several science fiction writers who have dealt with this problem. They handle history in a tachyon-consistent way when confronted with characters who can travel back and forth in time.
>
> For example, in *Behold the Man* by Mike Moorcock, Jesus turns out to be a twentieth-century time traveler who is so interested in the crucifixion that he goes back to watch – and gets crucified.

> Did you hear the one about the bloke who inherited his genes from his son?

Einstein made an oft-neglected statement shortly before his death, and in the presence of one of our SITU members. This was to the effect that he had never said that the speed of light was the ultimate possible speed for anything and everything. Rather, he said, it appeared to him from his mathematical analysis of reality to be only a "turnover" point; and for photons only, as far as he knew.

In simple terms, this means two things. First, light could surpass this turnover point; and, second, "other things" could do so without "turning over." Photons apparently have no existence until they start to move. We just wonder if they (or anything else, for that matter) are ever at rest in the first place.

This is pertinent to the further question as to what happens to photons eventually. Do they accelerate comparatively slowly and so surpass the speed of light, or do they come to rest and just cease to exist?

Or do they go on forever around our semi-visible universe? Do visual images spread out at the speed of light, and go on forever, or do they eventually vanish or become otherwise absorbed?

These hypothetical tachyons – "tachy" means "quick" in Greek – present us with a somewhat different hypothetical question, as outlined in the above quote. Just what might photons carry? Time? Gravity? What we call "mentality?"

Do all photons hit this turnover point? Does their future then become their past, or vice versa?

The essential point is, just what happens if photons (i.e., "superluminal" particles) can, indeed, exceed the so-called "speed" of light? Does your backside catch up with your frontside, and then keep going, so that you become inverted? And if so, would you then be going backwards in time?

In either case, what's the net result?

Well, it may be too soon to tell. If science fiction writers have already conceived of the "results" of quantum physics studies into photons, then the photons would seem (at least to this old-fashioned philosopher) to have made the jump already. They may, in fact, be constantly bringing back "information" from the far reaches of the universe. This may form a type of control system, modulating the thinking and preferences of all living creatures.

We seem to be becoming excessively ontological, but this item, too, falls within the Fortean purlieus of reality. Ontology encompasses cosmology, taxonomy of knowledge, and the ultimate basics of space, time, and locus. Year by year, unexplaineds both great and small are falling into an increasingly recognizable pattern. The clue to the whole business would now appear to be the thing we call "time," which we have grossly misinterpreted until now.

In *Science*, Vol. 171, p. 1228, Allen L. Hammond presented an article entitled "Stellar Old Age III: Black Holes and Gravitational Collapse," in the regular section entitled Research Topics. This starts off by saying: "According to the present understanding of stellar evolution, dying stars that are too massive to become white dwarfs or neutron stars collapse into what are called black holes."

There has been a lot published on this mysterious phenomenon in scientific journals, the science columns of newspapers, and some of the better popular magazines. It is an abstruse and highly technical matter. The average layman, even if deeply interested in the sciences, may well have given up on it after the first paragraph, as it is not one that can be made readily understandable without calling upon quite a lot of knowledge of cosmology, astronomy, physics, and nucleonics.

We do not presume to attempt an exposition of this ourselves, for even if we felt competent to do so, we would never be able to get a clear up-to-date statement into a quarterly – things are moving too fast. On the other hand, we feel we should bring to your attention certain aspects of what has been published about these black holes, which are of material interest to Forteans. We have not seen these better or more lucidly expressed than in this article.

Unfortunately, these aspects bring us squarely back into the distressing field of time anomalies, or "transitions." Hammond explains:

> Black holes were so named because no mass or light can escape from them, but it has become clear that as much as half of the energy of "rotating black holes" could be extracted.
>
> Apparently there are four kinds of black holes. The simplest – named after Karl Schwarzschild – has no charge and is not rotating. The more complicated geometry that results in the second type, which has both mass and angular momentum, was first worked out by Roy Kerr. This type of black hole has

> an inner surface known as the event horizon, from which no light or mass can escape, and an outer surface known as the stationary limit.
>
> These two surfaces coincide in the Schwarzschild type. A third type of black hole is characterized by mass and charge. The most general type, the fourth, combines all three properties – mass, charge, and angular momentum. According to Wheeler and Ruffini, transitions are possible from one form of black hole to another by, for example, the accretion of particles.
>
> The interiors of black holes are believed to have some remarkable properties. Inside the outer surface of these collapsed objects, for example, distance and time switch roles, according to the theory. Distance becomes a timelike coordinate, so that the distance of the particle from the center of the hole must always decrease, in the same way that time must go forward under ordinary circumstances.

These quotes are admittedly "out of context," but they are not invalid, as a perusal of the whole article will prove. The point is that what we call "time" can behave in a manner other than that which we have thought until now.

If time can be stretched, slowed down, distended, or inverted – the implication being that it can also be dilated or sped up – a great many enigmas could be explained.

CHAPTER 17

LATERAL RETHINKING – JULY 1972

Experiments (by whom or where not specified as yet) are alleged to have discovered that the eye is a differential organ, which can only see an image if it is moving *relative to* the retina. It ensures this by a continual irregular tremor at around 100 Hz.

Further remarkable experiments, in which this frequency is optically detected and used to vibrate the scene, exactly in phase with the viewer's eyes, have also allegedly been performed. This cancellation of the tremor maintains the image exactly static on the retina, such that the viewer cannot see anything!

But then, if a single tunable frequency (say, 51 Hz) is superimposed on top of this continual servo-tracking movement, the world immediately becomes visible again, for the optical image is now oscillating at variance with the retina.

Remarkably, if the experimentee looks at something at exactly the 50 Hz frequency (half of 100 Hz), the two frequencies will beat on his retina at the same time. For one half cycle, the image will be out of phase with his retina and moving over it, and for the other half cycle, in phase and moving with it. The experimentee will see the scene or object appearing and disappearing once a second.

This brings up some interesting possibilities. How about UFOs causing such in-phase interference? It would be the simplest thing to do, either unidirectionally or throughout 360 degrees, so that some individuals would see them flashing on and off, or just plain coming on and then later disappearing, while vast crowds could be similarly influenced.

This has nothing to do with what UFOs are, or where they come from; it is merely a rather solid new suggestion as to how they might appear to us to perform one of their "tricks." The same suggestion has been repeatedly made to explain their alleged ability to switch car engines and other electrical circuits on and off and, what is more, leave the engine running after they turn their gizmo off.

The following article is reprinted with permission from the January/February 1972 issue of *Flying Saucer Review*, and is by Colin Bord. We do not know whether the book he mentions, *The Use of Lateral Thinking* by

Edward de Bono, is available in the U.S., but we consider Mr. Bord's article most important. It is addressed to ufologists, but all Forteans should take heed. To wit:

> One of the current internecine squabbles among UFO researchers revolves around the question: Should Fortean and paraphysical phenomena be considered as having some value in our efforts to solve the UFO problem?
>
> While the advocates of this approach point out that UFOs are but one of the many enigmas with which we are surrounded, and may in fact be only part of a far greater mystery, the opponents feel (to quote from a recent issue of *BUFORA Journal*) that there "are enough fringe phenomena already classified or included under the UFO umbrella, which have no proven *direct* connection with UFOs."
>
> The author's italics for the word "direct" brought home to me the tenor of his thinking. Here was the traditional scientific approach to the problem – logical and exact, from one solid step to another solid step. This is the only recognized way with which to approach any problem, and the method we are all taught to use throughout our early years of training.
>
> But there is another type of thought-pattern that can be used – not one opposed to logic, but complimentary to it. This mode is used instinctively by those who feel that the Fortean and paraphysical are well worth considering. It is the mindset of the inventor and the originator – the individual who, to the envy of his fellows, appears to be able to pluck a cohesive coherent idea from what had seemed to be trackless confusion.
>
> This approach has been critically examined and defined, and termed "lateral thinking" by Edward de Bono, in his recent book *The Use of Lateral Thinking*. Traditional logical thinking he has termed "vertical thinking," and likens it to using building blocks, each block resting firmly and squarely on the block below it; whereas in lateral thinking, the blocks are scattered around, and the ensuing pattern can have a multiplicity of directions of approach, some of greater value than others.
>
> Lateral thinking is more concerned with possibilities than with certainty, and with the generation of new ideas, rather than the refinement of old ones, and so this book should be essen-

tial reading for every student of UFO phenomena. Indeed, sentences and paragraphs leap from the page as one reads; it could well have been written with the present state of UFO research in mind.

Thus we read of "dominant ideas" that can exert a "powerful organizing influence on the way a person thinks and approaches a problem." Or, again I quote, "It is disturbing to think how many situations are incompletely understood, because attempts at exploration persist in using well-tried familiar patterns, which ought themselves to be reexamined."

Although this is not a book about UFOs, in another sense it is very much concerned with them. Not only will it help us to question our mental approach to the problem, but it also shows us how to develop and use other patterns of thinking, which may pay greater dividends when applied to the UFO enigma.

I end with a quote from the book that might suitably be printed on thick card and sent to every UFO researcher:

> It is not possible to dig a hole in a different place by digging the same hole deeper. Logic is the tool that is used to dig holes deeper and bigger, to make them altogether better holes. But if the hole is in the wrong place, then no amount of improvement is going to put it in the right place.
>
> No matter how obvious this may seem to every digger, it is still easier to go on digging in the same hole than to start all over again in a new place.
>
> Vertical thinking is digging the same hole deeper; lateral thinking is trying again elsewhere.

MORE ON MERCURY ENGINES

Through the courtesy of our Adviser for Cultural Anthropology and Linguistics, Professor Roger W. Wescott of Drew University, we have received the following valuable information on the ancient Indian vimanas (flying saucers) and the first fully documented translation of a reliable Sanskrit text, published by a recognized scholar.

All the texts that we have had in the past have been pronounced to be "shoddy" by the scholars to whom we submitted them for translation. Also, in this new extract, the much more vital matter of the mercury engines crops up again.

Said extracts are from *The Yantras or Mechanical Contrivances In Ancient India* by V. Raghavan, published in 1956:

> The *Samarangana Sutradhara* ascribed to King Bhoja is, in many ways, a rare treatise in Sanskrit literature; besides the *Arthasastra*, it is the only theoretical text that has substantial information on our subject; its value, however, is greater than that of the *Arthasastra*, as Bhoja goes into the details of the construction of these yantras, and explains the principles underlying yantras.
>
> The most curious of the yantras described by Bhoja is, of course, the one that rises and travels in the air. The only text that gives us some knowledge of its actual construction is this work of Bhoja.
>
> Firstly, Bhoja mentions the main material of its body as light wood, laghu-daru; its shape is that of a huge bird, the *mahavinhanga*, with a wing on each side.
>
> The motive force is then explained. In the bowels of the structure, below, is to be a fire-chamber with mercury placed over a flame. The power generated by the heated mercury, helped by the concurrent action of the wings (which are flapped by a rider inside), makes the yantra go up and travel far.
>
> A heavier Daru-vimana is then described; it contains four pitchers of mercury over iron ovens. The boiling mercury ovens produce a terrific noise, which is put to use in battle to scare away elephants. By strengthening the mercury chambers, the roar could be increased, so that by it, elephants are thrown completely out of control.
>
> This specific military use of aircraft against elephants tempts one to suggest that the "Hasti-yantra" advocated by Kautilya (against elephants) was something like the heavier Daru-vimana described by Bhoja.
>
> There may be some lacunae in the description, and Bhoja does not fail to mention that some vital knowledge is kept back as

> a secret – an idea which we noticed in the *Brihatkatha* story also. It is, however, clear that mercury vapor ought not to be confused as providing any lifting power; it was evidently converted into mechanical power. The machine must have risen, as is expressly stated here, by the flapping of the wings. Further movement must have been due to the manipulation of the wings and the flow of air itself – as in the flight of birds.

This may come as somewhat of a depressant to the ET buffs and saucer boys, since they seem to have gained the impression that vimanas were huge, wingless craft that could fly not only over a bunch of elephants, but also out into space. The flapping wings as a means of gaining lift will be a disappointment to the engineers, and probably provoke wry smiles among them, to say the least.

But to a whole new breed of scholars that has only recently arisen, it is going to give much cheer and impetus to their various studies. These are the historians of technology, who are working out of a dozen cultural centers scattered around the world, all of whom are bringing to light an increasing flow of actual (tangible) artifacts that are either themselves technical devices, or scale models of such, dating all the way back to the late Paleolithic era.

That the Ancients did have knowledge of flight can no longer be denied. However, the Indians alone offer us concrete written information on power sources for them.

The Near Eastern items would appear to be gliders or sailplanes, though one Roman blandly states that he made his model "fly by compressed air." (Who, I ask, was compressing air in 200 A.D.?)

The South American types probably would not fly without power, but we are having copies of these tested in a NASA wind tunnel because, if they can do so, we will have one of the greatest breakthroughs in aerodynamics yet.

One ancient Egyptian item is the most exciting and confusing of all because, while it has the conformity of a glider, its fuselage looks more like a heavy-lift cargo plane the U.S. military now has on the drawing boards, but which is still full of bugs.

However, here we are more interested in the "engines" that are alleged to have activated these aerial machines.

In the January 1969 issue of *Science*, two scientists, Gerald Schubert and J.A. Whitehead, described a remarkable discovery they had made about heating mercury. On filling a wide, shallow, circular dish of mercury, and then revolving a naked flame around and around under said dish, they observed that the mercury began to revolve in a contrary direction, and with increasing velocity.

The most interesting thing in the above abstract, to us, is where did all the noise come from? Was this from just the mercury, or from some machinery it drove?

We must assume that this was part of the "secret," and so we shall never know, unless somebody with an eye to this mystery spots something in a text by a renegade technician. The Indian princes seem to have maintained whole stables of such purely practical, working technicians and, presumably, labs for them to work in. A few writings by such have been found giving rather intimate details of other "machinery."

If they had flying machines, did they invent them and their power sources themselves, or is this still another hint that there was once a much older and even more advanced, worldwide civilization that left a residue of its knowledge with native priesthoods?

Now that we know somebody was mining iron ore in 40,000 B.C., it looks more and more as if the old "ancient astronaut" theory may have validity.

Be it noted that the first of the metals to corrode is steel, and the last is gold. As we dig down, we find ultimately only gold copies of these vimanas and other machinery (those made with other metals having disintegrated).

Strangely, these gold figures (airplanes, etc.) are most competently made, and so seemingly advanced that archaeologists have either overlooked them for what they are (representations of actual planes and machinery), or have deliberately set them aside.

CHAPTER 18

OUTSIDE INTERFERENCE WITH HUMAN VISION – OCTOBER 1972

In our last issue, we reported briefly on some astonishing discoveries made on the incessant vibrations of the human (and presumably those of other animals') eyeballs. This showed that only rather slight electromagnetic or sonic interference from outside, if deliberately applied at a very specific frequency, caused volunteer experimenters "not to see."

We went on to suggest that this might be one of the methods employed by the UFOs or their operators.

Our member, Bob Durant, who seems to be becoming our leading light in analyzing the technical aspects of UFOs, sent this report:

> [That eyeball article] in the last *Pursuit* presents a hypothesis that could account for purely visual anomalies, but it seems a bit much to expect the vibrations to operate on mechanical devices such as auto engines, which are not frequency-sensitive in the same sense that the eyeball is.
>
> However, if the vibrations are basically of an electromagnetic nature, and thus give rise to powerful alternations in the ionization of the surrounding atmosphere, one might get both the physical vibrations necessary to accomplish the eyeball vibration *and* certain "induced" electromagnetic effects [on machinery].
>
> All of this is consistent with known laws of physics. The brain can be affected in specific ways by electrostatic fields. A strong EM field can give rise to visual hallucinations and also disable electrical/mechanical equipment.
>
> But I have yet to see the explanation for the restarting of auto engines. Stopping an engine is a simple matter – cut off the ignition. But starting is something altogether different, in that it takes a force to rotate the crankshaft. Simply restoring the ignition will do nothing.

This brings us back to time anomalies. If the UFOs use time as a means of travel, it is reasonable to suppose that the time field is deformed in the vicinity of the device. Thus the cars were running all the while, but during a peak in the time-flow deformation (caused by the UFO), time "stood still," and the engine *appeared* to stop running. With the departure of the UFO, time regained its normal properties, and the engine continued to run.

This is analogous to a stop-motion photo showing a car on a road. The photo preserves one instant in the motion of the car. We know that the car is in fact moving on the road, but the photo preserves one instant of its motion. Since we are familiar with cars and photography, all this is clear to us in the photo analogy. But in the case of the UFOs we are dealing with a totally unfamiliar set of concepts.

We are becoming increasingly intrigued by one detail of the reports of cars losing and regaining power. It tends to support the idea that some UFOs can hold automobiles in some sort of electronic vacuum or time-lock.

Sometimes, before a UFO disables a car, the driver leaves the ignition on. But in other cases, the drivers say that they had turned the ignition *off* during the encounter. They only turned it on again *after* their engines had started up spontaneously!

The former is understandable, but not the latter. How do you start a car after its electrical system has been turned off?

SKULLDUGGERY, SCIENTIFIC STYLE

There have been numerous newspaper and some magazine articles on this subject, but the best we have seen is the following by Gordon Slovut, a *Minneapolis Star* staff writer. It also brings together all of the incredible machinations of the archaeologists since these skulls were discovered, ending with the extraordinary statement from the Smithsonian. It reads:

> After studying two human skulls found in Minnesota's Boundary Waters Canoe Area four years ago, archaeologists are still uncertain if the discovery has any significance. There has been speculation that the skulls – because they have very low foreheads and pronounced brows – may have belonged to some Neanderthal-like man, and therefore would be older than any other prehistoric human bones found in this hemisphere.
>
> Dr. Elden Johnson, Minnesota state archaeologist, said the other bones and artifacts found with the skulls – discovered by Norman Saari, operator of a Tofte Lake resort – were insuf-

ficient to set an age for the bones. Dr. Martin Q. Peterson, a University of Nebraska physical anthropologist, examined the skulls while he was at the University of Minnesota.

> He thinks the skulls do have very low foreheads, but "you wouldn't think it too unusual if you saw someone like this walking down the street." After Peterson checked the bones, they were sent to the Smithsonian Institution in Washington, D.C.
>
> Dr. Lawrence Angel, curator of physical anthropology at the Smithsonian, said he had no record of the bones there, although he was "sure they were not lost." He said this means the bones probably are not an important find. "Plains Indians had skulls matching the description ('low-vaulted with pronounced brows') used in a report of the Minnesota find," Angel said.

Another version of July 11th, released by AP, states: "The skulls are under study at the Smithsonian Institution in Washington, D.C., and if Dr. T. Dale Stewart determines the skulls are unique enough to warrant further investigation, a Carbon-14 age test will be made. The test requires burning one gram of bone material, and University of Minnesota scientists have been reluctant to destroy any of the material."

That a carbon dating was not made immediately before contamination set in is inexcusable, and one gram would not destroy anything! Apparently none of them wants a very early date to appear.

(There have been constant reports of Neanderthal-looking skulls cropping up for years, and from all over. One lot from southern California were almost "super-Neanderthal," surpassing even the largest-browed and flattened cranium skulls of early Neanderthalers from Europe. They were supposedly donated to a local historical society museum.)

But perhaps the most astounding thing about this report is Dr. Angel's statement. There has been a constant stream of accusations that the Smithsonian "buries" things it doesn't like, but this is the most blatant admission we have ever seen.

According to Angel, anything deemed "unimportant" is not properly catalogued at the Smithsonian! Also, his conviction that the Minnesota skulls are really "not lost" implies that there may be "two sets of books" at the hallowed institution. How can he know the artifacts are there if he has not seen them, or at least seen some secret record of them?

CHAPTER 19

UFOLOGY: CAN WE TICK OFF ANOTHER ONE? – JANUARY 1973

Before launching into this tirade, we would just like to thank *The National Enquirer*.

The subject of ufology was pronounced "dead" a couple of years ago, after Dr. Condon published his mad and expensive report on the subject. That gentleman stated in print that any further pursuit of this matter was not worthwhile from a scientific point of view. As he was more or less "official," the press tended to believe him, and the public went along with that.

The matter of UFOs just dropped out of the news.

However, it most certainly did not do so anywhere else. The foreign press, the small presses in the U.S., and literally hundreds of private citizens groups formed to follow up reports of these things. And the reports grew, by leaps and bounds, to a point almost of insanity.

It got to a point where we (this Society) simply could no longer cope.

We have tried to be helpful by passing the material we get on to APRO and NICAP, just in case they might not have encountered it otherwise; but we doubt very much that either of these organizations has been able to make use of said material – even though they are devoted to this subject only. (Please note that we are not making much use of it, either. A couple of scientists who visited our HQ recently estimated that we had about 10,000 different items in our files!)

Now comes this.

The newspaper with the largest circulation in the U.S. is *The National Enquirer*, a weekly. A year ago, it offered $50,000 to anyone who could produce concrete evidence that UFOs are real, and that they come from off this planet – "are not natural phenomena," as they rather naïvely put it.

Well, the year is up and they have received thousands of reports. They state in an article in their January 28, 1973 issue that they are now going into the procedure of careful, complete, and scientific appraisal of this mass of material, but went on to state:

> "There are reports that clearly cannot be explained in conventional terms," said Dr. J. Allen Hynek, former advisor on

> UFOs to the U.S. Air Force. "And many of the reports meet the scientific requirement that more than one witness describe the UFO."

This is as near as anybody of sane mind and scientific training can come with amongst the mass of material *The National Enquirer* has turned up: there would appear to be some cases that are satisfactory proof, to established and orthodox science, that 1) UFOs exist, and 2) that they do not come from this planet.

That's all we want, brethren!

As to where they do come from, may we be so bold as to say that we have the answer waiting (if we are asked), and we don't want any 50,000 bucks for it, either.

"YESU" OF THE DRUIDS

There has been a legend in the southwest peninsula of England (Somerset and Cornwall) and southern Ireland, throughout recorded history, that says the Palestinian Essene whom we call "Jesus Christ" visited and resided at a place (today called Glastonbury) in northern Somerset.

This is a matter of enormous historical interest, and not only to theologians. Just look it up in any encyclopedia.

Let us, however, leave the theological aspects out of the picture for the moment, and concentrate on the historical, with some reference to botanical matters.

Did you know that the flowering thorn tree is really the basis for this whole legend?

In Glastonbury (County of Somerset, England) – and only there (nowhere else in western Europe) – is found a thorn bush, which flowers twice a year, and almost exactly on Christmas and Easter.

The story goes that these bushes in that area are all descended from a staff left outside a hut by one Joseph of Arimathea, a prominent Hebraic and Roman official (who was also the uncle of Christ and his guardian), on one of his periodic visits to the tin mines of Britain.

The so-called "thorn trees" constitute the genus Crataegus (a member of the Rosaceae family) of which there are at least 150 full species and now over 900 sub-species, though most of the latter were developed in North America. The common species of Britain is Crataegus *oxyacantha* – of which there are also numerous and very distinct sub-species.

They are all shrubs or small trees with, occasionally, an old giant up to 45 feet. The original indigenous distribution of this species was apparently from northwestern Europe north to 62-1/2 degrees north latitude in Sweden; and then east, via the sub-boreal belt, all the way to farthest Siberia; and then back west again, north of the mountains to Asia Minor and down to North Africa.

However, there is another species, known as C. *praecox*, which flowers twice a year and is indigenous to the eastern Mediterranean – south of the distribution of the C. oxyacantha group.

So why is there only one tiny place in Western Europe where this species has become implanted; and why should seeds taken from there (crossbred or otherwise) fail to perform in other locales?

Next, there can in no way be any doubt that the Phoenicians and other Palestinians obtained a major part of their supply of tin and other metals from this area in the islands of Britain, which the Greeks called the Cassiterides, or "Tin Islands."

Therefore, who would wish to deny that a leading metal trader, such as Joseph of Arimathea, should have taken his adopted son, age 12, on a trip with him to the west?

As to whether or not this adopted son happened to be the man we know historically as Jesus Christ is another question; but since that person appears to have been missing from Palestine from the age of 12 until 30, there is no reason to suppose that it wasn't him.

Finally, as you will see from this journal (see *Pursuit* Vol. 5, No. 1, p.16), it has been suggested (by Colin Renfrew) that the most ancient monotheistic theological influences spread not from the eastern Mediterranean to the north and west, but in reverse: from the north and west *to* the south and east.

In other words, the late Neolithics, and especially the Celtic ecclesiastics (often erroneously call the "Druids"), *were the first monotheists.*

They would have been best qualified to teach a young Palestinian Essene a pure philosophy that he could develop and apply to his ministry when he went home.

The fascinating thing is that the Celts had an ancient Messiah belief. They called their great philosopher and teacher-to-be "Yesu."

Coincidence?

For now, we would just like to revive this fascinating legend, because if it is true, it would rewrite the history books and, along the way, explain a few things.

Our "exported" Celtic members here in the U.S. might want to check into this mystery. Do you feel a strange genetic connection to Christianity, passed through your ancestors' DNA? Are you occasionally compelled to read the Bible for no apparent reason?

Please bombard us with your observations. There's more to this legend than meets the eye.

CHAPTER 20

GIANT SKELETONS – JULY 1973

We won't even hazard a guess as to how many modern "Neanderthals" are barging around the country, "hunting" down a Sasquatch or Bigfoot, but we have a suggestion for them: Try tracking down some of the many giant skeletons reported from all over the place.

A recent article in *The Winnipeg Free Press* tells of the successful search for a fossil whale skeleton, originally found by a farmer in 1906. In 1963, a local historian mentioned this in a book, and Richard Harrington, curator of quaternary zoology at Canada's National Museum of Natural Sciences, spent a year tracking it down through old records.

It was found in a hayloft.

The Spring 1973 *North Jersey Highlander* includes an article by the editor, W. Mead Stapler, entitled "A Mystery in History." It concerns giant skeletons.

Mr. Stapler notes that *The Conservationist* (a publication of the New York State Department of Environmental Conservation) ran, in its January 1967 issue, a piece on "The Lesser Wilderness-Tug Hill" area north of Utica, in which the author discussed the finding of "skeletons of giants, with double rows of teeth in each jaw."

The History of Bedford, Somerset, and Fulton Counties, Pennsylvania by Waterman and Hopkins describes the finding of the "remains" of a people of "gigantic size" who preceded the Iroquois, in an area about 100 miles south of Tug Hill. They were called the "Allegwi" (or "Alligewi") by the Iroquois.

In Benjamin J. Lossing's *Field Book of the Revolution* there is a footnote:

> [The author] saw, in the possession of Mr. Neilson, many relics plowed up from the battlefield [at Saratoga], such as cannon-balls, grape shot, tomahawks, arrowheads, buttons, knives, etc. And among them were some teeth, evidently front ones, but "double."

The teeth were attributed to the Hessians, but undoubtedly this is simply the result of propaganda.

Here's one from *The New York Times* of December 2, 1930:

> Discovery of apparent remains of a race of giants has been made at Sayopa, Sonora, a mining town 300 miles south of the Mexican border. J.E. Coker, a mining engineer, reports that laborers clearing ranch land near the Yaqui River dug into an old cemetery where bodies of men, averaging eight feet in height, were found buried tier on tier....

The above report was summarily dismissed by Bernard Brown, curator of the American Museum of Natural History, as pure exaggeration. Yet there is no indication that he ever saw the skeletons.

Here's another one from *The New York Times*, February 14, 1936:

> Managua, Nicaragua – Press accounts say that the skeleton of a gigantic man, with head missing, has been unearthed at El Boquin, on the Mico River, in the Chontales district. The ribs are a yard long and four inches wide, and the shinbone is too heavy for one man to carry. "Chontales" is an Indian word, meaning "wild men."

A third example from *The New York Times*, June 9, 1936:

> Miami, Florida – A tale of human skeletons eight feet long, embedded in the sand of an uninhabited little island off Southern Florida was brought here today by three fishermen. They exhibited a piece of one skull containing six teeth.
>
> E.M. Miller, zoologist at the University of Miami, said the mandible was that of a man and was probably several hundred years old. "It is entirely probably that this find might be important," he commented. The men said that the skulls were unusually thick, the jaws protruded and the eye sockets were high in the head.

One of our favorite tidbits has to do with the fact that some of these giants, in addition to having double rows of teeth, also had *horns*! (Yes, like the devil!) Will we be finding ancient pitchforks soon?

Robert R. Lyman reports on such matters in his delightful book on Pennsylvania's Black Forest, *Forbidden Land*:

> Eight hundred and more years ago, giant Indians with horns roamed the Black Forest of Pennsylvania beneath giant trees.

> At Tioga Point, on the Murray farm, a short distance from Sayre, in Bradford County, an amazing discovery was made. Dr. G.P. Donehoo, State Historian and a former minister of the Presbyterian Church in Coudersport, together with Prof. A.B. Skinner of the American Investigating Museum, and Prof. W.K. Morehead, of Phillips Andover Academy, uncovered an Indian mound. They found the bones of 68 men that were believed to have been buried about the year 1200.
>
> The average height of these men was 7 feet, while many were much taller. On some of the skulls, two inches above the perfectly formed forehead were protuberances of bone, evidently horns that had been there since birth. Some of the specimens were sent to the American Investigating Museum.
>
> We have more evidence that very tall men once lived in the Black Forest. In December 1886, W.H. Scoville, of Andrews Settlement, discovered an Indian mound at Ellisburg. When opened, the skeleton of a man was found. It was close to eight feet in length. Trees on and around the mound indicated that burial had been made at least 200 years before.

These are only a few of the reports of giant skeletons that have been found, and in many cases, said to have been sent to local museums.

Writing to museums, or even puttering about in their basements, may not be as exciting as tramping through the woods, but it is far more likely to produce results.

Quite a few Bigfoot and Abominable Snowman hunters have told us that they spent time "in the field" and saw nothing, but very often had the feeling that they were being watched.

In fact, one group was told by a forest ranger that he (the ranger) had seen a Sasquatch trailing them! Like most, they came home empty-handed.

Skeletons in museums or barn lofts won't run away, but they must be searched out.

Local museums are more likely to have specimens "buried" in their collections than the big institutions. Many of the larger institutions are operated by orthodox scientists and tenured academics, neither of whom want to have to rewrite any textbooks.

Small museums, in many cases connected with a local historical society, often depend on part-time volunteer help. Such persons are usually very knowledgeable, and certainly more interested in preserving the true history of their local area.

While we are on the topic, it should be noted that any large-scale administrative cover-up process works something like this:

1. Troublesome items become prone to losing their labels.
2. Unlabeled items soon have no value, and are therefore thrown out.

This process is not just limited to museums, however.

Nomenclature is an important part of our overall societal taxonomy (system of classification). The naming and renaming of things has always been a factor in our personal psychologies and philosophies, and plays an increasingly important role in politics, business, and science. Unnamed items and issues remain in the "unconscious" and are thus "invisible," leading to bloody scuffles in "the marketplace of ideas."

CHAPTER 21

PRE-EARTHQUAKE PHENOMENA – OCTOBER 1973

One of the things that interested Charles Fort was the occurrence of various phenomena preceding earthquakes, almost invariably dismissed by the "experts" as being "unrelated" to the quake.

Despite this, the common man has continued to report such things as glows in the skies, odd dark clouds, etc., before earthquakes. This has now become almost "respectable," because of the near necessity for finding some way to predict earthquakes, so that at least some precautions can be taken, or arrangements made to provide relief for the victims afterwards.

A recent earthquake in Mexico was preceded by flashing red glows, similar to "heat lightning," and sounds of thunder in a clear blue sky. White flashes were seen after the quake.

Soviet scientists studying the 1966 earthquake that wrecked Tashkent have announced that the sky there did glow for several hours before the quake, and that the cause was a "redistribution of electric charges in the earth-atmosphere system."

Electron concentrations were measured at stations at Alma Ata and Tashkent the night of the quake. The ionosphere over Alma Ata was found to be "calm," but over Tashkent "a silent storm of electrons" broke out several hours before the quake, reached its peak before the first tremor, and then subsided.

We have reported before on the fact that animals show every evidence of sensing an impending earthquake, despite a lack of obvious warning signals, and have speculated that some electromagnetic disturbance may be at the root of this. Humans also have the necessary "receptors," but these are either atrophied or we have trained ourselves to ignore the signals.

If you read reports by persons who have had some type of "psychic" experience, you will often find a statement to the effect that the episode frightened the person so much that he or she does not want anything like that to happen again, and will deliberately try to "block" such abilities.

This could be true of more "physical" predictions as well. (It would seem that few premonitions have to do with pleasant events.) Some very bizarre and measurable phenomena occurred before the earthquake that hit Hawaii on the 26th of April 1973 – so bizarre that one scientist said, "It's too much like Buck Rogers; we have no explanation for it yet."

About an hour before the earthquake struck Hilo (on Hawaii Island, some 200 miles southeast of Oahu) the radiowave-reflecting layer of the ionosphere some 50 miles up "suddenly disappeared – that is, for some odd reason, the layer did not reflect radiowaves sent up from the ground."

And the Navy's "Omega Navigational System," producing long wavelength (ELF) radio signals to guide ships far at sea, "began drifting and not making any sense." "Omega" hit its maximum drift just about the time the quake occurred, and then began to recover; and the ionosphere again began reflecting radiowaves immediately after the quake.

Discovery that the ionosphere went "missing" was a serendipitous outcome of studies set up to try to provide an early-warning system for tsunamis (tidal waves).

Major tsunamis are commonly preceded by a particular type of earthquake shockwave – called Rayleigh waves – which are detectable in the atmosphere as well as in the ground, and it was these Rayleigh waves that the observatory at Oahu (which discovered the "missing ionosphere") was looking for. They can be detected by special radio signals, and it was these that failed to return from the ionosphere.

The Hawaii earthquake was also abnormal in that tremors at Oahu continued to be recorded for two hours, instead of the usual 30 to 45 minutes. The reason for this is unknown. To date, so far as we know, there has been no published speculation on just what happened here, or why.

The widespread reports of flashing lights in the sky prior to earthquakes may indicate that "electron storms" are a common event in conjunction with earthquakes. In the articles available, there is no mention of such before the Hawaiian quake, but obviously, something went "wrong" with the ionosphere.

On the other hand, it would appear that the ionosphere over Tashkent, though disturbed, did not disappear before or during the 1966 quake. Nevertheless, there now seems to be no question that there are unusual atmospheric concomitants to earthquakes, and we would suggest that scientists pay more attention to reports from "natives" regarding bizarre effects preceding or following earthquakes.

The basic mechanism governing the occurrence of quakes is fairly well understood; what we need now is a thorough study of the less visible factors, symptoms, and consequences. Flashing lights are far from being the only unusual phenomenon reported before earthquakes.

THE CHINESE PYRAMID

One of the tantalizing stories we have been working on is that of an enormous pyramid in China, far exceeding, in size, any in Egypt or elsewhere. Our member Ron Dobbins has found several of the initial reports in *The New York Times* and a photograph of a pyramid from a book published in 1902. *The New York Times* article, in a UP dispatch datelined Shanghai, March 27, 1947, reads in part as follows:

> A giant pyramid in isolated mountains of Shensi Province in western China was reported today by Col. Maurice Sheahan, Far Eastern director for Trans-World Airline. From the air, Colonel Sheahan said, the pyramid seems to dwarf those of Egypt. He estimated its height at 1,000 feet and its width, at the base, at 1,500 feet.
>
> The pyramid, he said, is at the foot of the Tsinling Mountains, about forty miles southwest of Sian, capital of the province. A second pyramid, he continued, appears much smaller. The pyramid, Colonel Sheahan went on, is at the far end of a long valley, in an inaccessible part. At the near end, he said, are hundreds of small burial mounds. These can be seen, he said, from the Lung Hai railroad.
>
> "When I first flew over it, I was impressed by its perfect pyramidal form, and its great size." Colonel Sheahan said. "I did not give it thought during the war years, partly because it seemed incredible that anything so large could be unknown to the world. From the air, we could see only small footpaths leading to a village at the site of the pyramid."
>
> The Chinese have said that because of the almost complete absence of communications, even trails, in some parts of the West China mountains, it was not impossible that a huge pyramid might have been long forgotten [by the outside world].

The article goes on to note that Dr. James L. Clark of the American Museum of Natural History and Dr. Arthur Upham Pope of the Asia

Institute both considered the discovery to be one of "great scientific interest."

Dr. Pope, in a letter to the *Times* dated March 30, 1947, said: "This raises the further question, whether it will not perhaps verify the Chinese tradition of their first Hsia Dynasty, which it has been fashionable among Western sinologists to question. The next dynasty, the Shang, beginning about 1700 B.C., was long rejected by Western scholars also, until Chinese excavations at An-Yang established it beyond further doubt."

The Hsia Dynasty is now accepted as real. The latest dates that we have for it are 2205-1766 B.C. (traditional), and 1994-1525 B.C. (scientific). But it is incredible to us that after the An-Yang discoveries, there has ever been any doubt that *something* must have preceded the Shang (or Shang-Yin) Dynasty.

The Shang Dynasty is noted for its exquisite bronzes, which certainly were not developed overnight, and suggest a long period of sophisticated technological growth. In any case, Pope speculates that such a pyramid might be a Hsia royal tomb, and notes that it would be "one more demonstration of the Asia-wide importance of the cosmic mountain and the astro-celestial cult of which it was a central feature."

Mr. Dobbins, using other references not specifically listed in his letter, says:

> The Great Pyramid of Shensi is interesting – a virtual manmade mountain at 1000 feet high. This dwarfs the so-called "Great Pyramid' at Giza, which is about 470 feet high by 765 feet on the baseline.
>
> Despite the claims of discovery in 1947, the Georgia psychic and healer "Doc" Anderson visited the thing prior to the war and testified to its size. He claimed that it was made of earth or clay, and had a leveled top, on which perched the ruins of some kind of temple. Apparently the locals wouldn't let him get a closer look.
>
> And, apparently, it is located near the "field" of smaller pyramids. This group covers an area of some ten square miles – possibly more pyramidal structures here than in all the rest of the world put together, and all oriented on the north-south line, like the Egyptian examples. These Chinese pyramids have not been dated yet, but I wouldn't be too surprised if they are also the oldest.

Unless one wishes to call both Col. Sheahan and Doc Anderson liars, it is necessary to accept their photos, etc. as evidence that there are, indeed, enormous pyramids in China.

The largest artificial mound in Western Europe is Silbury Hill, near Avebury in England. It is 130 feet high, with a base covering more than five acres – small compared with the Great Pyramid, but still representing an enormous amount of labor, and, because of its earthen construction, closer in style to the Shensi Pyramid. Silbury's age and purpose are unknown, with shafts dug at various times revealing no burials or chambers of any kind.

Enquiries sent to the Chinese on a number of subjects have so far gone unanswered, but we shall try again to see whether they have changed their minds about the existence of these pyramids, and whether anything at all has been done about them.

THE BULGARIAN CYCLOPS

A UPI report of August 7, 1973 was headed "Cyclops Skeleton Found in Bulgaria" and read as follows:

> Bulgarian archaeologists have unearthed the skeleton of a "Cyclops" while excavating near the town of Razlog in the southwest of the country, the Bulgarian news agency BTA said. A brief report said the skeleton, which was found in a burial place, was 5 feet, 8 inches tall, and had only one eye socket in the coronal bone above the nasal cavity.
>
> According to Greek mythology, the Cyclops were a race of giants with single eyes in the middle of their foreheads. BTA said the unique discovery was made in the ruins of a building of unknown age, and specialists were making a thorough study of the remains.

Several of our members have asked if we have any further information on this, and the answer is "not yet." Inquiries have had to be sent to the Ministry of Foreign Affairs in Sofia, and this may take some time.

"Cyclopean skulls" dug up in various parts of Europe in past centuries were in fact those of elephantines, in which the nasal opening was mistaken for an eye socket. In the case reported above, the entire skeleton seems to be available, and definitely human.

There have been accounts of cyclopic individuals with one eye in the middle of the forehead in medical literature, but these are very rare and, so far as we know, limited to infants who survived only a short time.

Such a deformity is generally accompanied by other, usually lethal, defects, but it is possible, of course, that it could occur alone or with non-lethal abnormalities; and if the report given above is accurate, this must have been so here.

The full size of the skeleton would indicate that, if deformed, he must have been looked on as a "good luck charm," rather than something to be done away with at birth. Both attitudes have been recorded by cultural anthropologists.

CHAPTER 22

SAUCER NUTS AND VOLTS – APRIL 1974

Do "nuts" see "saucers?" This is the conventional thinking on UFOs, or was until recently, when a Gallup Poll revealed that a majority of the American public thinks that UFOs are real.

An enormous amount of damage has been done by the proponents of a theory that those who report unidentified flying objects, and those who take the subject seriously, are in some way mentally unbalanced.

Unfortunately, a great many members of the working press have adopted this view and used it to editorialize on their newspaper accounts of sightings. Usually this has been done in a humorous manner, but the message has not been lost on those who were unfortunate enough to be the subjects of the joke.

The attitude of the press has changed considerably in recent years, but it appears that there are still a few left who hold to the "nut" theory.

One such is Mr. Harry Reasoner, a prime-time newscaster on a major television network. Mr. Reasoner was recently featured in an advertisement in *The New York Times* and on billboards, which ascribed much wry profundity to him. Presumably the viewing public can again be cajoled into tuning into Reasoner for more of the same condescension towards those who are "different." It reminds us of those bad old days when each newspaper UFO story started out with "It's the silly season again..."

Mr. Reasoner quoted the Gallup Poll figure that 51 percent of the American public believe that UFOs are real. He also quoted Gallup's latest figures on the President's popularity – 27 percent. This, concluded Reasoner, might mean that we need a new President, but it certainly means that we need a new American public.

End of profundity from Mr. Reasoner.

Doctor Berthold Schwarz, a psychiatrist practicing in New, Jersey, has been a member of the SITU since its inception. He has addressed the question of the connection between "seeing saucers" and mental illness directly, and found that no such correlation exists.

If "nuts" see "saucers," it should be a rather common thing for a psychiatrist to encounter patients who are obsessed with thoughts about UFOs, or dreadfully afraid of them, or in communication with them, or whatever.

But, as Dr. Schwarz relates in his paper, this is simply not his experience in treating nearly 3,400 individuals with mental problems. Nor could anyone recall such symptoms in the records of the 30,000 patients institutionalized or treated, since 1900, at the Essex County (NJ) Overbrook Hospital.

The following quotes are from Schwarz's article from *The Journal of the Medical Society of New Jersey*, August 1969, Vol. 66, No. 8:

> In thirteen years of private practice, in which I have seen 3,391 patients in psychiatric examinations and have participated in thousands of hours of psychotherapy, I have never noted symptoms related to UFOs. A similar finding was confirmed on questioning Theodore A. Anderson, M.D., a senior psychiatrist, and Henry A. Davidson, M.D. (then Medical Director) of the Essex County Overbrook Hospital.
>
> Dr. Davidson recalled no patients with gross UFO symptoms out of three thousand in-patients, nor among all those presented to the staff while he was superintendent, nor of thirty thousand patients who had been hospitalized since the turn of the century. My own check of standard textbooks and journals in psychiatry, psychoanalysis, and neurology also confirmed this absence of UFO-like experiences in various "nervous" and mental diseases.
>
> This absence is remarkable, as the physician can (or should) be among the first to obtain reports of possible UFOs, and to uncover hidden cases, because a patient will often turn to a family doctor as a trusted friend.
>
> With the kind assistance of colleagues and friends (as a hobby outside of my practice) I have learned of, and studied, numerous well-documented UFO sightings involving people from all walks of life, including professionally trained observers, such as physicians, engineers, psychologists, airline pilots, special police, and state troopers.
>
> I have found no correlation between their sightings and mental illness.
>
> Their favorable "close-range" circumstances support the validity of the experiences. The witnesses were healthy and trustworthy. They had no gross defects of vision or hearing.

They had ample time to observe the UFOs. There was nothing suggestive of mal-observations, behavioral aberrations, mass hypnosis, contrived posthypnotic suggestion, or fraud.

The unique characteristics of the episodes and the backgrounds of the witnesses excluded such explanations as satellites, airplanes, balloons, helicopters, or birds. There was nothing suggestive of a parapsychological explanation in any of the examples.

Most of the witnesses were frightened and had a vivid memory of their unique experiences. It was possible to see how easily mass panic could have developed. The physician, by having an awareness of UFOs, can help to avert mass hysteria.

The cases I have investigated come from a relatively circumscribed area in northern New Jersey. They are but a small sample of the thousands of documented accounts from all over the world. UFOs indeed, do seem to be real.

Physicians are in an excellent position to uncover "hidden reports" of UFOs and help to establish the reliability of the witnesses.

By study of the possible emotional and physiologic effects of the UFOs, and of the witnesses themselves, the physician can go beyond merely establishing the event, and contribute to the more meaningful questions of: 1) what UFOs actually are, 2) where they come from, and 3) their purpose (if any).

CHAPTER 23

MYSTERY ANIMALS – APRIL 1974

Ivan Sanderson, the founder of SITU, was a zoologist of considerable accomplishment in that science, who worked for many years "in the field" collecting specimens for the British Museum of Natural History.

Perhaps as a natural outgrowth of this professional specialty, Sanderson developed an intense interest in "unknown" animals – that is, animals reported on numerous occasions, but as yet uncaught and unclassified. His writings on the subject stand as the definitive scientific work on unknown animals, and the Society has continued to collect data to further his pioneering work on unknown animals.

The bipeds commonly known as Yeti, Sasquatch, Bigfoot, etc., and the Loch Ness Monster are the best known of these anomalous animals, though they represent only a fraction of the total number of reported "unknowns" on record.

In very general terms, there have been three major explanations put forward in an attempt to account for these reports. The first holds that the reports are the result of misidentification of known animals, or simple frauds and hoaxes. (For an example of this, see *The Encyclopedia Britannica*, under the heading of "Abominable Snowman.")

The second explanation, which seems to be the consensus of most students of the subject, is that the animals are indeed real, and in most cases are well known to the indigenous "natives," but that they have merely avoided being caught to date.

The third explanation is to the effect that the reported animals are the product of some paranormal or even extraterrestrial agency, perhaps ghosts or phantasms.

It is interesting to note that the adherents of all three theories recognize the fact that despite considerable effort, we have yet to capture a specimen of any of these animals. Of course, each group explains this rather embarrassing fact in accordance with its own idea of the nature of the beasts.

Group One says that one can't very well capture something that is not there in the first place. Group Two asks us to wait a while. Group Three seems to believe that the phenomenon is, by nature, so far removed from our usual understanding of the words "animal" or "capture" that capturing one is a practical impossibility.

This we shall examine in more detail later on, and not merely as an exercise in liberality, but because some of the keenest students of monster reports have collected an impressive amount of data that we feel deserves careful consideration, regardless of how bizarre this theory may sound at first glance.

Most Abominable Snowman (ABSM) hunters are very firmly of the opinion of group number two. We have had the opportunity to ask a number of them, including some genuine professional "big game" trappers, why they suppose it has been impossible to capture an ABSM.

They are fairly unanimous in the opinion that capturing a large, extremely strong, extremely swift, and most importantly, presumably intelligent animal (such as the ABSMs are reported to be) is a most difficult task.

What follows is a gross oversimplification, but when setting about trapping any animal, one must first learn the habits of the animal. Then a hunting scheme, based on the animal's habits, is formulated. Finally, the hunter must be a very patient and diligent fellow.

The popularly held view of trapping, featuring a mob of fashionable people roaring off into the bush in a caravan of Land Rovers, or with a string of "natives" carrying heavy bags and equipment, is strictly "Hollywood." The native assistants on rare-animal hunting expeditions are valued mainly for their intimate knowledge of the terrain and the habits of the hunted animal, rather than for their strong backs.

To sum up, it is the opinion of the "pros" that ABSM hunts have been lacking in most, if not all, of the essential ingredients: sufficient manpower, sufficient staying power, and, most especially, an adequate knowledge of the creature's habits.

This was brought home to us in a very vivid manner several years ago, in a nearly tragic event that made headlines throughout the country.

A young couple had been picnicking in a state park with their nine-year-old mentally retarded son. Sometime during the afternoon, the boy wandered off. His parents searched for several hours for the lost child, and were eventually forced to call for help. By nightfall, over four hundred searchers had been assembled and were combing the area.

At daybreak, helicopters and light airplanes were pressed into the search.

The aircraft and key personnel on the ground were in constant two-way-radio communication. The boy was spotted a number of times, both by aircraft and members of the ground party, and at times was seen no more than 50 yards away.

Nevertheless, he managed to avoid capture. After three days, the boy surprised one of the searchers by walking directly up to him, in a clearing, and asking for help.

The moral for ABSM hunters – especially for those who are inclined to dismiss the subject because we have not yet captured one – should be quite plain.

More recently, a crocodile was the subject of a large-scale search in a small, shallow lake in Florida. This one was finally caught, but only after three weeks of "Keystone Cop" chases through the clear water, and the combined arsenal of grappling hooks, nets, electric shock, and baited buoys. All of this was to no avail.

Finally, the temperature dropped to 30 degrees, and the croc decided to end the game by leaving the water for a sunbath.

Little wonder, then, that Nessie has avoided capture in the depths of Loch Ness, where the water, even a few feet below the surface, is nearly opaque with suspended particles of peat.

All of this makes fine sense to us, but we are nevertheless forced to admit that a number of cases of unknown animals present an array of most unsettling circumstances that would seem to require an "unnatural" explanation. In these cases, the animals apparently share some characteristics with what have come to be known as "ghosts" – though what "ghosts" are is something we don't know at all.

To be specific, the tracks of these animals seem to suddenly appear, meander about in a "normal" fashion, and then disappear. The animals themselves often inhabit a small area for weeks or even months, but eventually disappear just as suddenly as they appeared. Sometimes they glow in the dark, or glowing objects are seen near them.

Ordinarily courageous, fierce dogs absolutely refuse to track them. It is claimed that in a number of instances, the unknown animals have been seen immediately after the appearance of UFOs, such as in the upper Ohio Valley (Pennsylvania, Ohio, and West Virginia) last year. There are even reports of UFOs depositing and collecting animals and creatures (e.g., "Mothman" flying in or out of a UFO).

During the 1973 Ohio Valley flap, large "cats" (variously described as pumas, cougars, panthers, etc.) were commonly seen alongside UFOs and ABSMs. Strangely, in the few instances where the witness was qualified to make a fairly precise identification as to the species of the animal, the anatomical details have been strangely inconsistent with those of any known animal.

Often these visitations are accompanied by the widespread slaughter of livestock and other domesticated animals. Indeed, there are many instances in which such depredations have been the only indication that an animal was about. Some of Charles Fort's most chilling stories concern the panics caused by these "mystery cats."

Janet Bord has been keeping track of "mystery puma" reports in England, and has furnished us with a compilation of newspaper accounts. Just a little investigative "legwork" can yield a wealth of detailed information about these strange appearances.

U. S. ARMY ENDORSES BIGFOOT

Bigfoot has received something of an endorsement from the U.S. Army Corps of Engineers. The latest issue of the Washington Environmental Atlas, a compendium compilation of a variety of data concerning the environment of the State of Washington, mentions Bigfoot as one of the ecological features of the State:

> The very existence of Sasquatch, or "Bigfoot" as it is sometimes known, is hotly disputed. Some profess to be open-minded about the matter, although stating that not one piece of evidence will withstand serious scientific scrutiny.
>
> Others, because of a particular incident or totality of reports over the years, are convinced that Sasquatch is a reality. Alleged Sasquatch hair samples inspected by FBI laboratories resulted in the conclusion that no such hair exists on any human or presently known animal for which such data are available.
>
> Information from alleged sightings, tracks and other experiences conjures up the picture of an apelike creature standing between 8 and 12 feet tall, weighing in excess of 1000 pounds, and taking strides of up to 6 feet. Plaster casts have been made of tracks showing a large, squarish foot 14 to 24 inches

in length and 5 to 10 inches in breadth. Reported to feed on vegetation and some meat, the Sasquatch is covered with long hair, except for the face and hands, and has a distinctly humanlike form.

Sasquatch is very agile and powerful, with the endurance to cover a vast range in search of food, shelter and others of its kind. It is apparently able to see at night and is extremely shy, leaving minimal evidence of its presence. Tracks are presently the best evidence of its existence. A short film of an alleged female Sasquatch was shot in northern California, which, although scoffed at, shows no indication of fabrication.

The Pacific Northwest is generally considered to be the hotbed of Sasquatch activity, with Washington leading in number of reports of tracks or sightings since 1968. However, reports of Sasquatch-like creatures are known from as far away as the Parmir Mountains in the U.S.S.R. and South America.

If Sasquatch is purely legendary, the legend is likely to be a long time dying. On the other hand, if Sasquatch does exist, then with the Sasquatch hunts being mounted, and the increasing human population, it seems likely that some hard evidence may be soon in hand. Legendary or actual, Sasquatch excites a great popular interest in Washington.

(The full report is available through the U.S. Government Printing Office.)

CHAPTER 24

THE COUNCIL OF NINE AND OTHER ANCIENT MYSTERIES OF PUBLISHING – OCTOBER 1974

Just as Bigfoot, Nessie, and flying saucers have captured the public's imagination in this century, the subjects of pyramidology and Lost Atlantis enthralled millions one hundred years ago. Both have since declined, overshadowed by the seemingly more provable speculations on monsters and extraterrestrials.

But small bands of scholars, intermingled with the inevitable crackpots and con artists, still pursue the futile game of guessing at the hidden meanings in the pyramids, and engaging in the romantic search for a long-lost "Ancient Astronaut" supercivilization.

The literature on both these matters is now both voluminous and wearisome. So, Charles Berlitz's exhaustive examination of the Atlantis myth is as refreshing as an open window in a smoke-filled room.

Originally published in hardcover in 1969, *The Mystery of Atlantis* has been updated by its author for the paperback edition, and contains a succinct review of some of the new discoveries of the past few years.

Are the peculiar stone constructions in the waters off the Bahamas remnants of Atlantis? Or was Atlantis in the Mediterranean, as some modern scientists now claim? Did the massive pillars discovered 6,000 feet under the Pacific Ocean, off the coast of Peru, belong to Atlantis? Or was Atlantis near the Azores, as some people believe?

Mr. Berlitz examines all the lore and evidence, carefully weighs the complaints of the skeptics and beliefs of the advocates, and then chooses sides. Atlantis is really out there somewhere, he has decided.

Berlitz, a very successful author, spends part of his busy life exploring the mysterious underwater world of the Bahamas. Thus far, his efforts have produced little more than a quality suntan and this highly readable book.

If you have room on your crowded bookshelves for only one Atlantis tome this year, this should be your choice. (Your big comfy reading chair could become a "chariot of the gods," particularly if you add a stiff martini!)

In other news, Andrija Puharich's *Uri: A Journal of the Mystery of Uri Geller* was published. Puharich, best known for parapsychological work on

CIA-funded subprojects (his experiments in Mexico, using mind-altering drugs on ESP subjects, were featured on national television), goes for broke in this "cryptic" tale.

Uri (pronounced Oori) Geller, for the benefit of those who have been in a coma for the past year or so, is a young Israeli who apparently possesses rather extraordinary psychic abilities, and has demonstrated his talents both for the public (on stage and TV) and for the Stanford Research Institute. This is his "authorized" biography of sorts.

The book comes in two parts, though these are intermingled. One deals with Geller's abilities as such, and the investigation of his alleged powers of telepathy, psychokinesis, etc. There has been a great deal of controversy over this, with some investigators claiming the he is a charlatan doing "tricks" that any good magician can do, and others insisting that his powers are genuine.

The truth may lie somewhere between these two extremes, but it certainly seems that he does have some abilities that must be considered paranormal. On the basis of the information in Dr. Puharich's book, it is impossible to draw any final conclusions here, but it must be pointed out that if even one percent of the deeds attributed to him are genuinely paranormal, he is worth further investigation.

The other part of the book deals with Andrija Puharich's ideas on the nature of Geller's powers, and the way in which he acquired them. To put it mildly, this makes rather extraordinary reading. In the Epilogue, Puharich says, "The reader must be the judge of whether or not I have succeeded (in convincing you that my story is true); to which I must reply, 'Sorry, chum, but I don't believe a word of it.'"

Andrija Puharich has done some very solid work in the field of the paranormal, and his two previous books (*Beyond Telepathy* and *The Sacred Mushroom*) are straightforward and relatively discerning. He was responsible for bringing Peter Hurkos to this country and performing carefully controlled experiments with him and Harry Stone.

Puharich also has over fifty papers in scientific and professional journals to his credit. In short, one would expect a reasonably scientific approach to a study of Uri Geller and his abilities.

Unfortunately, Puharich sounds like a classic "contactee" here, although he more or less denies being one. Puharich claims that all of his journals, films, and materials concerning Geller were confiscated by Israeli Intelligence when he left Israel, and there is no indication that they were returned to him later.

This does not prevent him from quoting long conversations, and giving names, dates, places, and times down to the exact second. At the very least, one must credit him with a phenomenal memory. (He states that he started writing the book, *without* the journal, in February 1972.)

He first met Uri in Israel in 1971, and conducted a number of experiments with him. Initially, these seem to have been as well controlled as was possible in the circumstances. This happy state of affairs does not appear to have lasted very long.

Puharich's principal thesis is that Uri Geller is "the ambassador for an advanced [extraterrestrial] civilization" and that he, Puharich, has been chosen as the "principal witness ... and chief scribe." It is not clear how Uri came to be chosen for this role, inasmuch as he does not even seem to impress Puharich, very much, as a person.

Puharich calls him an "unabashed egomaniac" (p.87), and though he grants him "honesty and boyish charm," he also notes his "small-minded approach to life, an almost desperate hunger for security and recognition" (p. 208), and quotes an Israeli friend who says they "have a word in Hebrew for a kid like Uri: 'puscht,' which means 'punk' in English. He is really insufferable."

Nevertheless, another friend considers him an "early stage Old Testament prophet," and Puharich clearly has no doubts about the roles they have been called on to play, while admitting freely that he has not one iota of evidence to back him up.

In what seems to have been a kind of pseudo-psychiatry designed to wean Geller from his blatant materialism and introduce him to his own soul, Puharich asked permission to hypnotize him. Uri's answer (p.89) was "That's easier said than done. I'm in show business; many hypnotists have tried to hypnotize me, and nobody can. It just won't work."

However, he gave Puharich permission to try and was told (p.93) that "even though he was going to be hypnotized, he would remember everything that happened in this first session."

Geller was asked to count backward from twenty-five, and by the time he reached eighteen, "he was in a deep hypnotic trance." When he awakened (p.95), "he could scarcely believe that he had been under hypnosis for an hour and a half. He had no memory of what had occurred."

It was during this hypnosis session that the extraterrestrials first made themselves known to Puharich – who told Geller all about it.

Their message was that they (the extraterrestrials, given various designations such as Hoova, IS, Rhombus 4D, etc. depending on the particular branch of the civilization doing the talking) had found Uri in a garden when he was three years old, and had "programmed him for many years to come, but he was also programmed not to remember. On this day his work begins. Andrija, you are to take care of him."

The message was recorded on a cassette tape, which vanished from Uri's hand when he grabbed it (while it was being played back for him). From this time on, his paranormal powers were even more remarkable than before.

Unfortunately, all of the most spectacular feats were witnessed only by Geller and Puharich and, in a few cases, by others who can legitimately be called Geller's disciples. This hardly constitutes evidence.

As for the messages from the ETs, every single tape on which a message was recorded either vanished completely, or was mysteriously and instantly erased. This is either frightfully significant or frightfully convenient. The messages have, however, been transcribed from memory by Messrs. Puharich and Geller.

Like all other communications from space people, these are not very helpful; in fact, they are seldom intelligible and occasionally contradictory. After informing Puharich that they will "silence the atomic weapons of the world," they show a distinct tendency to urge him to "pray" for peace. They also note that they "can command any communication system man has devised" (p.124), but "cannot contact you directly" (p.174).

According to Puharich, the universe is controlled by "The Nine," under whom there are other sub-controllers (called Controllers). Then there are the messengers, some of which take the form of UFOs. And finally, as the intermediary with Earth people (the only one for the next fifty years) is Uri Geller. The problem is that either The Nine or the Controllers (I forget which) is/are a computer.

It is not clear where this computer (or bank of computers) is located, but it exists some millions of years in the future. One of their ways of making themselves known and impressing Puharich and Geller was to indulge in such constructive acts as moving 7-Up glasses (the old, upside-down kind) around.

How they have managed to program this (to be triggered by Uri) from their vantage point millions of years in the future, is, again, not clear, and even Uri on one occasion exclaims: "But look at the foolish things they are doing to us. It looks like they are not stable, goddamn it..."

To which one can only add: "Amen, brother."

Uri, by the way, is to help not just Earth, but also the universe (p.124). "Spectra" (another of their names) has told Puharich that "there are some books on your planet left by our people. Uri will find them in the years to come. Your questions will be answered. They [the books] will materialize themselves away, after they have done their work" (p.114).

The future sounds awfully convenient!

Now, I am probably guilty of a certain facetiousness, so I must make it clear that I have not the slightest doubt that Dr. Puharich is utterly sincere, and believes every word in the book. I have been told by a very reliable informant that approximately 30% of the original manuscript was deleted by the publisher, because it concerned Andrija Puharich and they wanted a book on Uri Geller.

This is understandable but unfortunate, since one would like to know a great deal more about Puharich and his "conversion," particularly in view of some rather disturbing elements here.

It is stated (p.284) that Puharich founded Intelectron Corporation "to develop electronic systems for aiding hearing in nerve deafness, and holds 56 U.S. and foreign patents for his inventions. He has also applied for patents on his systems to enhance ESP."

At one time, he was under contract to the Air Force to develop a miniaturized radio receiver that would fit into a tooth (it is not known whether or not he succeeded, and there is no evidence at all that he ever took Uri to a dentist).

He seems to have (or have had) an extraordinary influence on Uri (p.66): "We met Geller after the show… He readily agreed to meet me at my apartment, the next day at 1 p.m., to discuss my research interests and find out what I wanted to do. I did not realize then how lucky I was. Later I found out that Uri had steadfastly resisted all offers by research people to do experiments. He, too, was surprised at how readily he had consented, especially since I was a total stranger."

Add to this the ease with which Puharich hypnotized the unhypnotizeable

Geller, and the implications are rather interesting.

Andrija Puharich is undeniably sincere and convinced that Uri is our intermediary with an advanced civilization, and is nearly paranoid about it when others fail to recognize Uri's "genius." He says (p.228) that Uri "felt the full weight of the lynch mob that was being organized against him in the U.S. My goal was simple: to keep the human race from talking itself into a crucifixion state of mind."

Geller knew nothing of his "mission" until Puharich told him about it, and the early messages from them arrived while Geller was in a hypnotic trance. Is Puharich perhaps an *unwitting* contactee, who is using the sometimes naive and pliable Geller to spread – as many others have – the bogus messages of the ETs? If he is, he could even be using his electronic expertise without being consciously aware of it.

As Puharich freely admits, there is not a shred of evidence for extraterrestrial contact, and there is no good evidence for Geller's most spectacular feats. Puharich even claims that many of Geller's standard psychic acts are not Geller's at all, but are the extraterrestrials acting through Geller.

Certainly the message being transmitted via Puharich-Geller is typical of messages from "space people" – and typically unhelpful at that. If there really are "space people" who are contacting certain persons on Earth, they must be as immature sociologically as they are (presumably) advanced, technologically. I personally believe we can do without their "help."

In the case of Puharich, perhaps he is a contactee, or perhaps he has, for reasons unknown to us, developed a kind of messiah complex, which he is indulging vicariously through Uri Geller.

I have spent a perhaps inordinate amount of space on this book, but in view of the intensive campaign being carried on by Dr. Puharich and the nature of his claims, I think a rather full exposition is needed.

Dr. Christopher Evans, writing in *The New Scientist* in April 1974, notes:

> [Puharich] is a broad-minded, tolerant, and sincere chap who, in my humble opinion, believes with the most blazing sincerity, every word in the book. This must be true, for no one prepared to sit patiently, listening to mediums relaying information from extraterrestrial scientists (who make remarks like "peace is the integral fruitage of personality"), could be anything but broad-minded and sincere – particularly when they write about it afterwards with such enthusiasm.

There are a number of points made in the book which are not even touched on here, but I believe I have given you fair warning.

CHAPTER 25

MEANWHILE, IN THE BERMUDA TRIANGLE... – AUGUST 1975

When zoologist Ivan Sanderson and I first discussed the Bermuda Triangle publicly, on the Alan Burke television show in 1967, we were flabbergasted by the audience reaction. As soon as the show went off the air, the switchboard lit up like a Christmas tree.

Sacks of mail poured in for weeks following the broadcast. Public interest seemed all out of proportion to the few short minutes we had spent describing some of the mysterious disappearances in that sector of the Atlantic Ocean between Bermuda and Florida.

Although author Vincent Gaddis had published some excellent summaries of the strange events that had occurred in the Triangle a few years earlier, the general public had apparently never heard of the phenomenon, and was hungry for more information.

Sanderson later carried out an in-depth research project into the mystery, and published his findings in 1970.

In the past couple of years, several books have appeared, all borrowing heavily from the pioneering research of Gaddis and Sanderson, and some of these books have become national bestsellers. Public interest in the Bermuda Triangle is at an all-time high.

It has become a common topic on radio and television talk shows. Each new disappearance in that area (and there are several each year) is now headlined in newspapers from coast-to-coast and sensationalized in the tabloids.

Whenever a Fortean subject becomes this popular, critics quickly appear. So it is not surprising that books debunking the mystery are now beginning to flow into the bookstores.

Those same learned gentlemen who once told us that flying saucers are nothing but swamp gas, weather inversions, and meteors are now informing us that the planes and ships that have vanished in the Atlantic without a trace – not even leaving an oil slick behind – were the victims of ordinary storms and natural occurrences.

Ivan Sanderson spent weeks laying out the known disappearances on maps, and consulting with engineers and scientists. He discovered that the Triangle is really lozenge-shaped, and that there are 12 of them equally spaced around the world. Some of these areas have been known for centuries and are surrounded by superstition.

One lies just off the coast of Japan, and has long been known as the Devil's Sea. The government of Japan decided to get to the bottom of the mystery in the 1950s. A special ship was outfitted with the latest scientific instruments and equipment, and a crew of scientists sailed into the Devil's Sea to solve the puzzle. The ship and its entire crew vanished completely, without a clue! Today, Japanese fishermen go many miles out of their way to sail around the area.

Both the Bermuda Triangle and the Devil's Sea share one factor in common: both are pierced by magnetic "agonic" lines. An agonic line is a geographical line along which magnetic compasses point to true north. In most places on this planet, compasses deviate from true north by as much as 20 degrees.

These deviations have been carefully measured and charted, and are known as "isogonic" lines. For example, the isogonic line in northern Maine varies by 20 degrees, while in Texas, the isogonic line is 10 degrees off. Pilots and navigators take these deviations into account when they are charting their courses.

The North American agonic line begins at the western tip of Lake Superior in the north, wends its way through Illinois into Kentucky, Tennessee, and Georgia, and passes into the Atlantic from the tip of northern Florida – where the dreaded Bermuda Triangle begins.

For years now, pilots in that part of the Atlantic have been troubled by peculiar magnetic aberrations. There are several "dead spots" where radio signals cannot be transmitted or received. Since modern pilots depend heavily on radio navigation, these dead spots can pose serious problems. A flier heading for Florida from the Bahamas can suddenly find himself cut off from all communication with the mainland.

At the same time, his compass often starts spinning senselessly, and his other navigational aids also malfunction. He can find himself flying by the seat of his pants, even though a well-equipped airport is only a hundred or so miles away. Some pilots have, understandably, panicked and started flying in aimless circles until their fuel was exhausted.

If these dead spots were stationary, it would be possible to investigate them and maybe figure out what causes them. But, unfortunately, they seem to move around like a radar beam being projected at this planet from another point in space. When they appear, these dead spots almost always straddle the agonic lines.

Flying saucer enthusiasts have talked about the electromagnetic (EM) effect for years. Pilots have often reported that their compasses have malfunctioned while they had visual contact with an unidentified flying object. It has been assumed that UFOs radiate powerful magnetic fields because of this effect. But it isn't that simple.

Because magnetic compasses are not very reliable to begin with, most airplanes are also equipped with gyrocompasses and other instruments such as the "artificial horizon," which also employs a gyroscope. Many of these gyro instruments are not electrical. A stream of air strikes the blades of a small, turbine-like wheel, which spins the gyro once the plane is in flight.

Such instruments should be absolutely impervious to magnetic interference, but they often malfunction at the same time that the magnetic compass goes haywire. Pilots in the Bermuda Triangle have reported that their gyro instruments have failed simultaneously with compass failure *and* radio blackouts in these dead spots! In short, these spots (and some UFOs) contain forces that are beyond ordinary electromagnetism.

MAGNETIC ANOMALIES

For centuries, sailors have observed and charted magnetic anomalies all over the world. A small island in the Red Sea causes ships' compasses to spin crazily when they sail past it. Aircraft charts also record such anomalies. The charts for the Washington, D.C., area note: "Magnetic disturbance of as much as 8° exists at sea level in the Chesapeake Bay and Elk River from Latitude 39° 17' N Longitude 76° 16' W to Latitude 39° 30' N Longitude 75° 54' W."

But the dead spots of Sanderson's lozenges cannot be charted. They are in constant motion, and since they affect gyro instruments as well as compasses and radios, they must be made up of energies that extend beyond the normal electromagnetic spectrum. In many respects, these energies are more like the EM pulse that radiates from an atomic explosion, or the curious atmospheric anomalies that accompany earthquakes.

During an earthquake on a Pacific island a couple of years ago, scientists discovered that the normal atmosphere above the affected area seemed to open up and swallow radio signals. Signals that normally bounce off layers in the upper atmosphere didn't bounce during the earthquake. They just kept going upwards and were lost in space.

Similar "holes" over the Atlantic could produce the mysterious dead spots. Whether these "holes" are caused by geo-magnetic conditions or by something else remains unknown. If holes are somehow ripped in the protective atmospheric layers over the Atlantic, it is possible that other forces such as very intense cosmic rays could leak through and damage the machines and men caught in the dead spot.

Charles Berlitz, author of a bestselling book about the Triangle, has another theory. He speculates that fabled Lost Atlantis was once located in the Atlantic, and that it was populated by a technologically advanced race, who produced a powerful energy generator of some kind. When Atlantis sank into the ocean, the generator continued to function, and it is still out there under many fathoms of water, periodically sending out great waves of energy that have a destructive effect on the planes and ships passing over the generator.

Ivan Sanderson, Berlitz, and all the other Bermuda Triangle investigators have overlooked one astonishing fact. Sudden disappearances are not limited to those 12 watery lozenges. In fact, disappearances on land are far more numerous. Airplanes have disappeared without a trace over heavily populated New Jersey. Ships have vanished suddenly and inexplicably from the surfaces of small inland lakes and rivers.

Even automobiles have disappeared suddenly in Japan, South America, and the U.S. In several well-documented cases, drivers have suddenly found their cars enveloped by clouds of mysterious fog, and when it cleared, they were hundreds of miles away from the place where they had been only minutes before!

Pilots in the Bermuda Triangle area have reported this same kind of unnatural fog. One moment, they were flying through a cloudless sky in perfect weather; the next moment, they were in the midst of an impenetrable fog.

Even people *walking* have reportedly been engulfed by a fog that transposed them in space and time. We know very little about this bizarre phenomenon.

Fortean and UFO books recount dozens of mysterious land disappearances, some of them going back a century or more. You may recall that the great flying saucer wave of October 1973 began in Georgia – right on the agonic line.

You don't have to fly a light plane over the Atlantic if you want to join those who have disappeared. Over 20 major disappearances in recent years have taken place far inland, all on the agonic tine. And literally hundreds of unusual UFO sightings and events have occurred along the same agonic line.

The second most active line in the U.S. is the isogonic line marking a five-degree deviation beginning in Mississippi, in the south, and extending to Minnesota in the north. Not only have UFOs been uncommonly active along this line, but our strange giant, hair-covered creatures with blazing red eyes have also staged their appearances along the line.

In previous writings, I have discussed the apparent link between paranormal manifestations and magnetism. The clustering of manifestations along the agonic and isogonic lines is further proof that the earth's magnetism plays a very important part in all unexplained phenomena, from the sudden disappearances of people and objects to the sudden appearances of phantom cats, hairy monsters, and spooky spacemen.

If you live directly on the agonic line, you may be in as much danger from these unknown forces as you would be if you were sitting in a rowboat in the middle of the Bermuda Triangle.

The ancient Chinese and northern Europeans charted these lines of force, and constructed leys or "tracks" to mark them. Perhaps we should do the same.

Check with a local surveyor and find out about compass deviations in your area. You might make an interesting discovery. Perhaps you, like Ivan Sanderson, live in a place where a compass needle just floats in a circle.

But if you find that the needle points to true magnetic north, maybe you should consider moving.

CHAPTER 26

UPDATE ON FORTEANA – APRIL 1976

When Ivan T. Sanderson founded the Society for the Investigation of the Unexplained (SITU) over a decade ago, he put forth some very intelligent ground-rules, including a ban on "any aspects of medicine or psychology; the social sciences or law; religion or ethics." At that time, those subjects seemed remote from the Fortean interest in unknown animals, meandering nocturnal lights, geographic anomalies, and archaeological conundrums.

The past decade, however, has seen a dramatic change in the overall approach to these matters. Psychiatrists, psychologists, and sociologists are now deeply involved in UFO research. All of the once-strictly-physical sciences are merging into a superscience that is actively exploring so-called "inner space," as well as the visible universe. Even religion is being absorbed into this superscience.

Behind the closed doors of scientific academies all over the world, learned men are discussing parallel universes, antimatter, the possibility of extraterrestrial life, and the nature of reality itself. Realms that were once the exclusive domain of a handful of Fortean researchers are now public property. A golden age of Forteana has arrived with surprising and unexpected suddenness.

Ufology, once considered to be the hobby of cranks, has attained respectability. Popular books, such as the phenomenally successful *The Bermuda Triangle* by Charles Berlitz, are turning a large segment of the population into amateur Forteans. Television and motion picture documentaries on Fortean subjects are assaulting the public's senses. Newspapers are filled with sober accounts of new breakthroughs at Loch Ness, and in Abominable Snowman research. Occult subjects, sneered at a few years ago, are now being studied at major universities.

We could choose to ignore this explosion and go about our quiet way, collecting "angel hair" and cataloging the mischievous appearances of kangaroos in the American countryside. But this Society has become a recognized leader in the Fortean field worldwide. To maintain that leadership it must bend, if ever so cautiously, in the winds of change.

Certain aspects of psychology and parapsychology (or paraphysics) do belong in the pages of this journal. The exciting exploration of inner space has become a natural extension of our other interests. Even the important new studies of religious apparitions demand our attention.

During our first years of existence, SITU and *Pursuit* were dominated by Ivan Sanderson's towering intellect. Now that Ivan is no longer with us, we call upon all members and friends to contribute to these pages. In addition, we expect to offer articles by highly qualified, recognized authorities in all of the aforementioned interlocking areas of interest.

The sociological impact of UFOs may prove to be more important than the UFOs themselves. The psychological effects of monsters and sea serpents on their witnesses may provide us with the most valid clues to their exact nature. Fish falling from the sky may tell us something about the eccentric composition of space, time, and parallel universes.

Above all, a coordinated effort to explore all of these seemingly disparate fields, in a cohesive manner, may well uncover some remarkable new facts about the human race itself, and its ultimate place in the cosmos.

This is what our society, SITU, is all about.

THE MYTH OF UFO CENSORSHIP

On page 354 of Stephane Groueff's *Manhattan Project, The Untold Story of the Making of the Atomic Bomb*, one finds this quote:

> It was not known to the general public that during the war, the Japanese were attempting to fire balloons against the West Coast of the United States... About nine thousand "Fugo" balloons were launched, but, flying without control once they got up in the air, they were inefficient. The first two to be seen in the U.S. fell in Montana and North Dakota, and were reported in the Japanese press a week later.
>
> Since only local American newspapers had mentioned the incidents, Japanese spies were obviously reading the smallest country publications. After that, any mention of the balloons in American papers was censored out.

A magazine article by Air Force Major Robert C. Mikesh, dated June 28,1968, corroborates the above:

> On January 4, 1945, the Office of Censorship asked newspaper editors and radio broadcasters to give no publicity whatso-

> ever to balloon incidents. This voluntary censorship was adhered to from coast to coast, a remarkable self-restraint in a free-press-conscious country…
>
> Three months later, in a "strictly confidential" note to editors and broadcasters, the Office of Censorship stated: "Cooperation from the press and radio has been excellent, despite the fact that Japanese balloons are reaching the U.S., Canada, and Mexico in increasing numbers. There is no question that your refusal to broadcast information about these balloons has baffled the Japanese, annoyed and hindered them, and has been an important contribution to security."

Are all of the governments of the world deliberately suppressing reports of UFO sightings in the same way that the Office of Censorship (long defunct) managed to suppress news of the Japanese fire balloons during WWII? The cry of "censorship" was first raised by the late, lamented Fortean Society in the 1930s, long before the UFO "flap" of 1947.

Within weeks of the events of June 1947, the emerging groups of civilian UFO researchers clutched at this anarchistic banner and proceeded to trample across two long decades with it. The protests of "censorship" quickly jelled into allegations of a dark, sinister conspiracy, purportedly instituted by the government to keep the "truth" from the American people.

Over the years, bits and pieces of circumstantial evidence were added and weighed by the UFO buffs. The Air Force – not just the American Air Force, but all Air Forces – were made the villains of the "plot." Censorship ceased to be a mere suspicion; it became one of the "facts" of ufology. But how true is this "fact?" How much censorship actually exists, and how is it implemented?

As of 1964, there were 1763 major dailies in the U.S., plus thousands of smaller daily and weekly newspapers. That same year, there were 589 television stations, and 5350 commercial radio stations. These figures have naturally increased in the past five years. Most of these newspapers and radio and television stations are independently owned.

Many of these businesses are fiercely independent and anti-establishment. To issue any kind of censorship order, either in person or by mail, to all of these editors would be a formidable task. The Office of Censorship, which folded in 1946, had the personnel, political footing, and financing to do this; the U.S. Air Force does not.

What's more, the turnover of personnel in the communications media is traditionally very high, and any such "order" would have to be issued again and again, perhaps even semi-annually, to be effective. If such an order existed at all, it would quickly become common knowledge to newspapermen everywhere. And some maverick, anti-establishment editor in a "flap" area would almost certainly take the trouble to publish the order in its entirety.

I have been in the newspaper and publishing business since I was 12 years old, and I have never met an editor, reporter, or publisher who has even heard of such an order. Nor have I ever personally encountered a member of the news media who claimed to have been "silenced" by any kind of government agent or agency regarding UFOs.

Editors working near secret military installations, atomic energy plants, etc., are sometimes asked not to mention these installations in their papers, but this is a clearcut matter of national security. The newsmen willingly concede to such requests, just as they obeyed the balloon order of 1945. This is purely voluntary on their part.

God help anyone who tries to order a hardboiled newsman not to print something he feels really should be printed!

The clippings from both small-town and big city papers throughout the past twenty years also belie the censorship myth. During the yearlong flap of 1966 in New Jersey, the Patterson, New Jersey *Evening News*, and many other papers, carried almost daily box scores of UFO sightings. Many hundreds of local sightings have been given banner headlines in the large dailies across the country, all out of proportion to the actual merit of the incidents.

I have met many researchers who have collected huge files of clippings of the so-called "lull" years. The late Morris K. Jessup compiled an impressive yearbook based entirely on the published sightings of 1955, widely thought to be such a lull year. In 1966, I subscribed to several national clipping services, and was buried in thousands of clippings from local and national news media that year.

If somebody is being employed to censor UFO news, they should be given the sack immediately. They just haven't been doing their job!

For the past several months, I have been conducting an extensive nationwide poll of both UFO believers and skeptics, asking 77 key questions to determine their attitudes and beliefs. While I have not yet completed tabulating all of the results, some startling statistics are already apparent.

Over 15% of all the disinterested (i.e., non-UFO researchers) polled now claim to have seen an unidentified flying object. (Only 6% of those polled by Gallup in 1966 made the same claim.) But a whopping 65% of this same group said they believed the government was actively suppressing UFO information.

Nevertheless, in every state, and in every isolated area polled, the newsstands were glutted with UFO paperbacks and magazine.

The simple truth is that the UFO organizations and their members have been screaming about censorship for so long that today, a large percentage of the general public believes these allegations. To add to the mess, Air Force public relations have been grossly mishandled by bored, uninterested personnel (the Pentagon post of "Project Blue Book spokesman" is used as the last stop before retirement, so the turnover by officers there is very high).

We've heard a lot about the Air Force censoring its own personnel. But the big question is whether or not Air Force censorship actually goes beyond its own bases.

In February and March of 1968, I was invited to record two pro-UFO programs for the Voice of America (VOA) network in Washington, D.C. Mr. Al Johnson of VOA had done many pro-UFO shows for the government propaganda station, and they have been broadcast all over the world. He has interviewed everyone from government employees who have seen UFOs to the most controversial of the contactees. No Air Force officer has ever come around to snip his microphone cable.

Both the Pacific and European editions of the U.S. Army's newspaper, *Stars and Stripes*, also carry frequent UFO items, both pro and con. American troops overseas have been duly informed of everything from West Virginia's "Mothman" to "Snippy," the famous late horse supposedly mutilated by the ufonauts.

If governmental suppression of UFO information were a reality, it would stand to reason that the first media to be censored would be the Armed Forces Network, VOA, and *Stars and Stripes*. If those mysterious Air Force censors can't even shut up the governmental news organs, how in the world can we believe that they are able to silence *The Podunk Weekly Gazette*?

Those who have been loudest in accusing the Air Force of censorship have apparently never taken the trouble to discuss the subject with the editor of their hometown newspaper. Many of the "censorship buffs" have delightedly gone on local radio and television and discussed censorship for hours, without ever getting cut off the air.

When they managed to insinuate their names into the columns of the local press, and the editor or reporter chose to give their talk of "little men" and disappearing planes the tongue-in-cheek treatment, these same buffs have claimed that here, again, was proof that the press has been ordered to ridicule the subject.

Actually, the press has spent years ridiculing the ET believers, not the subject of UFOs itself. When a believer failed to say anything quotable, the reporter often tossed his notes in the wastebasket, for there was no story. But believers who opened up and chattered about blond Venusians and "Men in Black" were quoted – and justifiably ridiculed.

Flying saucers attained a high degree of respectability in the early 1950s. Major American magazines such as *Look*, *Life*, *Reader's Digest*, *The New Yorker*, and all of the glossy Sunday supplements carried lengthy articles that were very fair. In many cases, they showed outright enthusiasm for the subject.

At the same time, Captain Edward Ruppelt's brand new Project Blue Book struggled almost heroically with the contradictory data. Ruppelt is remembered for his honest dealings with the press. He didn't know what the answers were, he admitted, but the government was spending a million dollars a year trying to find out.

The loudmouths weren't satisfied, however. They wanted to read about new sightings every week. Frank Scully's controversial *Behind the Flying Saucers* hit the bestseller lists and the "little men" were fast becoming part of American folklore. Then the "contactees" broke noisily onto the scene with their tales of desert meetings with the Venusians. The Air Force censors didn't do a very good job of shutting them up, either.

The contactees lectured, wrote books, appeared on radio and television, and suddenly, it was almost too much for the bemused public to swallow. Perhaps if the contactees had bided their time, the subject would have grown steadily more respectable. The public, quite naturally, had to accept the reality of the unidentified objects before they could be prepared to accept the notion that someone or something might be riding around in them.

This was a very big emotional hurdle in the early 1950s. Nearly all of the learned astronomers of that period were still flatly rejecting the idea that there might be extraterrestrial life, and mainstream ufology was based upon the concept that extraterrestrial life not only existed, but was also visiting us daily.

The timing was extremely bad. In retrospect, it almost seems planned. We might shudder at the thought, but suppose the UFO occupants realized we were beginning to take them seriously; and suppose they did not want this. One way to counteract all of the favorable publicity would be to create situations that would bring ridicule to the subject again.

In any case, the somewhat premature appearance of the contactees – and the mind-shattering possibilities presented by their claims – produced automatic censure. Nobody was ready to believe backwoods farmers and disreputable amateur astronomers. So the press and the public turned against the funny contactees and their pseudo-philosophical cults.

Simultaneously, the CIA's Robertson Panel looked over the speculative and unsubstantiated material so painfully collected by Ruppelt and his men, and they ordered the Air Force to stop wasting money on something that could apparently never be verified or proven.

The Dark Ages yawned open again. Newspaper editors yawned, too. They'd been dealing with flying saucer stories since 1947, and nothing ever seemed to come of them. Now that UFOs were disreputable again – the new reports were often quite absurd – the editors became more and more selective about the stories they used.

Occasionally, an incident like the "little men" of Hopkinsville, Kentucky (1955) would capture the editors' fancy and be played up nationwide. But a story had to be almost outrageously silly before the newspapers would bother with it.

The UFO buffs must recognize several solemn facts about the newspaper business. First of all, the average small-city daily has from two to six teletype machines rattling away 24 hours a day, churning out miles of copy covering everything from the price of cloves in Zanzibar to the scores of high school basketball games in Eldora, Iowa.

A large part of the editor's paper is composed of advertising, comic strips, and local news. He has to be very selective about how he uses the remaining space. Important national news, ranging from wars to motion picture publicity, naturally takes precedent over "human interest" items. Flying saucers are human-interest items, like occasional yarns about haunted houses, sea monsters, and sensational murders.

Speaking of murders, there were an estimated 10,920 murders in 1966, according to the FBI. How many of these killings did you read about in *The New York Times* or the Emporia, Kansas *Gazette*? Perhaps only a dozen of these crimes actually made news nationally. Does this mean that crime news is being censored? Hardly.

I can speak with some authority on the UFO news of 1966, because I enlisted five major clipping services to supply me with every available flying saucer story that year. In addition, people all over the country and the world began to send reports to me. I collected over *10,000* for 1966; of these, sixty were given extensive national coverage by the wire services, and many of them were played up on the front pages.

Flying saucers had become more important than murder!

There were nationally publicized contacts, "little men" stories, police UFO chases, and military sightings. In addition, there was a sudden revival of interest on the part of national magazines.

A year or two earlier, a professional writer could not have stirred up interest in a UFO article in any editorial sanctum. Now, suddenly, every writer in New York was pouring over NICAP's *UFO Evidence*, and rewriting it for popular consumption. One-shots (single issues of special magazines) flooded the newsstands.

During 1966-68, no less than 46 paperback books suddenly appeared on the subject, covering everything from George Adamski to attacks against the Air Force. These books became available in every corner drugstore. Many of them followed the old ufological line and were harshly critical of the government. No Air Force sergeants ran from store to store, buying them up.

Two books, Coral Lorenzen's *The Great Flying Saucer Hoax* and Captain Ruppelt's *Report on Unidentified Flying Objects*, were ruthlessly rehashed by no less than four of my writer friends, the sales of which paid all their bills for six months. Another friend of mine wrote a quickie paperback novel based on the Betty and Barney Hill case, called *The Terror Above Us*, and was able to move to Tangiers on the proceeds.

Plagiarism, yes; censorship, no. If the government sincerely wanted to censor UFO material, they could have stopped this flood of material by quietly visiting no more than six or eight of the major paperback publishers. No one would have ever known.

But to show you how tenaciously the ET buffs cling to the censorship myth, look at the rumors surrounding the demise of the Dell magazine, *Flying Saucers – UFO Reports*. Dell had originally jumped on the UFO bandwagon with a single, competently edited rehash, intended as a one-time-only project. It sold so well that they put another issue together – three more, in fact.

Response from the distributors is slow, however, often taking from to two to four months. So, Dell editors were working on the fourth issue when the executives learned that sales on the second and third had fallen sharply in comparison to the first. Since this type of publication must sell at least 250,000 copies to break even, they realized they were in danger of selling less than that number by the fifth issue. So, being practical businessmen, Dell executives decided that there would be no fifth issue.

I contributed several articles to *Flying Saucers – UFO Reports*, and was on very good terms with the editor, Carmena Freeman. When she reluctantly announced that the magazine was no more, she was anxiously queried by students of the censorship myth, asking why this fine publication was folding. She inadvertently sent out brief letters in which she casually mentioned that the decision had been made by "the powers that be" – referring to her bosses at Dell.

The phrase ricocheted through all the UFO fanzines. "The powers that be" had shut down *Flying Saucers – UFO Reports*! The evil Air Force silencers had struck again!

There had been UFO one-shots in the early 1950s, too. Saucer books sold well for a while, and then interest died out. There is no mystery about it. One-shot publishers move with the fads. In the late 1960s, hippies became a fad. Then assassination became a fad. The newsstands were glutted with one-shots dealing with our recent national tragedies, as well as any lurid killings that might occur (particularly of an "occult" nature).

Before that, we had that tribute to abominable taste, called "camp." Everyone was being campy. Next month, bullfighting might be the thing – or kite flying.

Are the American bullfight aficionados crying "censorship" because their beloved and bloody sport is being neglected?

We must face it. Flying saucers are a "nut" subject. When the New York publishers smell growing public interest again, they will again flood the newsstands with rehashes of Lonnie Zamora's flying egg, and Captain

Mantell's premature demise.

The real UFO "hardcore" seems to consist of about 5,000 people in the U.S. Until 1966, and then only because of John Fuller's excellent efforts to popularize the subject, there was simply no profitable market for UFO literature. Overnight, a "softcore" of perhaps 500,000 people appeared.

This softcore has been buying up the quickie paperbacks, but they will soon tire of reading about Zamora and Mantell. Sales will drop off, and publishers will again avoid the subject. And when this decline does occur, there will undoubtedly be new cries of "censorship" from the myth-mongering advocates for "UFO Disclosure."

There is another kind of very real censorship, which has been reasonably approached by the ET buffs. This is the self-imposed censorship that takes place on the local level. I have encountered it continuously in my travels, and have commented on it briefly in some of my other articles.

On the magazine level, we find that many editors try to avoid the truly wild and unbelievable things now occurring nationwide. Some editors are still shy about contactee stories, unless they are given a humorous treatment. Others seek to maintain the tired old controversy about "Air Force suppression," because it has a strong emotional appeal.

Some editors do not believe in UFOs themselves, and so they demand that the subject be handled in a light, offhand manner. A number of editors have told me, "Oh, we did a UFO article last year. It's too soon for another one."

Only two nationally distributed magazines in the U.S. try to carry a UFO article in each issue! *Fate* has, of course, been following the subject for 20 years, but has a limited audience; *Saga*, a blood-and-guts men's magazine, has carried in-depth articles monthly for about two years. Most of *Saga's* pieces are written by Brad Steiger, Joan Whritenour, Otto Binder, and myself. We have all been doing comprehensive articles based upon our own personal investigations.

Some of the hardcore believers in Venusians have literally frothed at the mouth over our findings, which do not always fall into accord with their beliefs. It is rather ironic that the same people who have been crying for years, "Why doesn't somebody tell us what is going on?" are now whipped into a frenzy because a handful of us are actually investigating the subject firsthand, and are trying to tell them what is going on.

We have been accused of making up pure fiction by some of these groups, even though I long ago issued a standing offer: my files are open to any serious investigator. I will happily supply full names and contact information of witnesses to any ufologist who displays sincere personal interest and has a genuine desire to recheck my cases. So far, only six people have taken me up on this.

Many self-styled ufologists remain bitterly in the dark because they are actually unwilling to do anything more than read (and criticize) heavily edited summaries of complicated cases. Very often, the published article is so watered-down and condensed that it bears little resemblance to the original. Overly critical readers do not seem to be aware of this problem. It is not censorship. The cuts are usually made because of space requirements.

Newspaper articles are even more severely limited. And this self-imposed censorship is exercised to a very high degree. The average small-town editor does not want to willfully ridicule – or subject to ridicule – any of his subscribers. Thus, if a local citizen becomes involved in a UFO incident, the editor and the reporter involved are likely to be overly protective of their story.

A man might report, for example, that a glowing circular object landed in his backyard, and that a small, humanlike figure made a brief appearance. The published story might omit the man's name ("I don't want people to think I am crazy"), and nearly all of the other salient details. The clipping, when and if it ever reaches the ufologist, might merely state than an unidentified man reported seeing a glowing circular object near his home. Only by making a careful, firsthand investigation can the ufologist discover that there was a great deal more to the story.

The story was not really censored by anybody. It was merely reported in a cautious, superficial way. Furthermore, editors in flap areas usually do not try to keep up with all the reports they receive. Instead, they publish only a selected handful of those UFOs witnessed by police officers or local dignitaries (usually those containing the best descriptions).

You can receive a single clipping from an area, and when visiting the place, you might discover that hundreds of people have been seeing things.

At the height of the enormous flap around Harrisburg, Pennsylvania in 1967, the local newspaper coverage was very superficial. The same kind of scanty reporting took place around Ithaca, New York during the massive flap there.

The flap around the Savannah River Atomic Energy installation in South Carolina, also in 1967, was so intense that the local newspapers were literally stunned into silence. Editors and police officials decided not to publicize the flap. They figured that something big and important, possibly involving national security, was taking place. The Savannah plant, which is the size of the city of Chicago, manufactures nuclear weapons.

There is one cardinal rule that seems to take effect in every area involved in a major flap: the longer a flap lasts, the less publicity it receives. If a flap lasts for only two weeks, the local papers are more apt to carry daily reports, etc. (Incidentally, it seems as if somebody in every flap area always manages to get pictures, but these photos seldom filter down to the ufologists.)

If a wire service takes an interest in the flap, it may receive national coverage for two or three days (as happened in Michigan and Ohio in 1966). But the story "plays out" quickly. When the wire service drops the story, the flap has not necessarily subsided.

When the objects appear almost daily and are seen by hundreds, as frequently happens in flap areas in the U.S., people tend to take them for granted. After the initial expression of curiosity and interest, they cease to report their sightings to anyone. The published reports dwindle, but not the sightings.

Since most of the sightings tend to be very similar, the local editor gets bored with it all, and publishes fewer of the incidents that are reported to him or the police. "We get flying saucer stories all the time," is a common complaint. "We just can't print them all."

In many communities, the editor of the local paper may not regard the daily sightings as "news," so he simply doesn't print anything about them. Or, because they are so common, he may reason – as many people now do – that the objects are some "secret government project," and he probably should ignore them.

The average newspaper "investigation" into a routine sighting consists of a brief phone call between the reporter and the witness, or a brief interview. If the witness has seen something really unusual or, more important, experienced something unusual, he may not even give all of the details to the reporter, for fear of ridicule.

Thus, once again, the published story is merely a superficial account. It takes an in-depth interview by a skilled ufologist to obtain all of the facts in the case.

There is another type of case now common in the U.S. that should be mentioned. This is the "privileged information" type of incident, in which something extraordinary happens and the police or the witness – or both – ask the reporter not to write the story.

This is a very common procedure, and cannot be construed as censorship. Police often try to keep details about a murder, for example, quiet until they can have had a chance to investigate thoroughly, and follow up every clue. Usually, reporters and editors automatically go along with this, out of respect for the victim or witness.

By the same token, if an Air Force officer (or someone wearing an Air Force uniform) should turn up at a UFO site and ask reporters not to publish anything about the case at the time, the reporters are likely to obey. I have personally never encountered this, nor have I ever met an editor or reporter who has admitted to this kind of "silencing." Other American investigators have allegedly come across this sort of thing, however.

I have many excellent and baffling cases in my own files that I have not published, because I have been asked by the witnesses not to publish them. I don't regard this as censorship. If I were writing about the political scene, I would encounter this sort of thing much more frequently, I'm sure. The Air Force has never asked me to lay off anything, however.

You can see now some of the problems of relying on newspaper clippings for information. They serve only as a barometer for the situation, just as TV pollsters interview less than 2,000 families about their viewing habits, and on that basis, determine how many millions of people are watching particular shows.

A single bland clipping about a police officer in an obscure little town, seeing something odd in the sky, might be the tip-off that a big flap is in progress in that area. A three-paragraph story about an object hovering over a local water tower can easily cover up a landing or something even more sensational. A rash of clippings from a single place, followed by a sharp decline in reports, may actually mean that a truly enormous flap is occurring.

Based upon these patterns, we might even speculate about the alleged "lulls" of the 1950s and 1960s. Perhaps the "lulls" are really the periods of *greatest* activity.

For every published report, there may be hundreds or even thousands of witnesses who have never reported anything. In recent months, we have begun to uncover contact cases that purportedly took place years ago. The witnesses were either too afraid to speak out, or they didn't know who to go to with their story.

It is possible that UFO activity has actually remained at a surprisingly consistent level for many years, and that all of the "waves" are illusory, because they are based upon published reports, not upon firsthand investigations of affected areas.

In *The New York Times* of January 29, 1934, there was a report of "mystery airplanes" appearing nightly over Finland, Sweden, and Norway, and even London, England. This early Scandinavian flap might rule out all of the speculation that our atomic bomb blasts inspired the European episodes of 1946 and the American episodes of 1947 – the supposed "start" of the saucer age.

Point Pleasant, West Virginia, a little town engulfed in a massive flap from 1966 to 1968, also had UFO incidents in 1930 (*The New York Times*, December 31, 1930).

Nearly everyone agrees that the UFOs are some kind of vehicles. So it now seems reasonable to assume that those vehicles are active during flap periods, perhaps transporting personnel and material into the flap areas. Then, during the "lulls," when the objects are supposedly least active, the personnel carry out specific chores at ground level (the risky nature of the operation being "hidden" by declining news coverage).

If this hypothesis can be supported (and there is now a great deal of evidence to support it), then we must consider that the importance of the phenomenon is not found in questions like "Where do they come from?" or "How are they motivated?" It is: "What specific things are they doing in our rural areas, without detection?"

Newspaper clippings will never give us the answer. They will not even furnish us with the questions. As comedian Fred Allen once observed when criticizing radio and TV pollsters, it's like counting the grains of sand in the bottom of a birdcage, and trying to determine the size of the Sahara Desert from them.

The speculations about a governmental conspiracy to suppress UFO information was based largely upon the appearance and activities of alleged Air Force officers. There are far too many "silencings" stories to discount. I do not deny that real Air Force officers may have actually been involved in such activities, particularly in the 1950s.

Back in the days when the Air Force was taking the subject very seriously, and intelligence officers were directly involved in UFO investigations, it would have been standard operating procedure to try to restrict public information on cases under study, just as the police frequently try to suppress information about crimes being investigated.

But my personal experiences, and those of many other American researchers, strongly suggest that another, non-governmental group was – and is – involved in silencing UFO witnesses. In case after case, witnesses have told me of having been visited by "government men," who advised them to keep quiet about what they had seen.

Some of these witnesses were baffled, because they hadn't reported their sightings to anyone at that time, and they just didn't know how the government could have found out. When you pin such witnesses down, you usually learn that the men in question did not identify themselves at all, or they gave a vague identification.

In nearly every case, these men, including the ones in Air Force uniforms, are described in the same way: short (usually 5'6" to 5'9"), olive complexions or a "deep suntan," high cheekbones, and oriental caste to their features. This sounds uncomfortably like the common description for the UFO occupants…

Those ufologists who cling to the "benign extraterrestrial" theory find this to be totally unpalatable. Yet several other American researchers have now uncovered cases identical to my own.

We have a lot of facts going for us now. We know that the objects tend to operate most extensively in thinly populated areas. This alone suggests that the objects and their occupants are engaged in covert activities, and that they do not desire detection or discovery.

The next logical step would be to silence those who accidentally stumble upon their activities. The simplest and best method for achieving this would be to send agents to the witnesses, representing themselves as official government personnel.

Should this fail, sterner measures could be taken to discredit the witnesses. A witness could be coaxed into complaining to local authorities that his phone is being tapped, his mail is being tampered with, and that mysterious people in black cars are following him.

All of these things will brand him a paranoid. "That poor fool. First, he thought he saw a flying saucer, and now he thinks the government is after him," the authorities will mutter. "Looks as if he has gone around the bend!"

There is a degree of UFO "censorship," but can we really accuse the government – any government – of spending the money and devoting the personnel needed for such a huge and essentially pointless project? Who has the most to hide, and possibly the best reasons for maintaining the ridicule and the secrecy? The U.S. Air Force, or the occupants of the flying discs, cigars, and orbs that flit about, late at night, in dark and lonely sections of the country?

CHAPTER 27

RAY PALMER: UNSUNG UFO PIONEER – JUNE 1977

When they dare to step outside the narrow confines of their particular field or specialty, scientists nearly always become bumbling, undistinguished amateurs. Those who take up such hobbies as photography, magic, painting, or even candlemaking rarely gain even a modicum of recognition among their fellow hobbyists.

Today, talent and imagination are not prerequisites for a scientific career, but are actually a handicap. Old-style scientists such as Albert Einstein, Charles Steinmetz, Nikola Tesla, and J.R. Oppenheimer have become obsolete. A new breed has appeared in recent years – an elite of technicians rather than innovators.

How many living scientists can the average person name today? And how many of them have made viable, definable contributions to the human condition?

Science has become a world of gadgetry, designed to foster product development and increase corporate profit. People have been forgotten amongst the computers and machines of the scientific-industrial complex.

For many years, the myth persisted that once "science" recognized the UFO problem, the mystery would be solved, and many universal questions would be put to rest. But in actual practice, scientists have an appalling record in ufology, beginning with the schizophrenic, multimillion-dollar investigation subsidized by the U.S. Air Force.

Time and again throughout the 1950s and '60s, whenever a man with scientific credentials entered the UFO fray, he succeeded only in spreading unnecessary confusion and conflict. Nothing productive was ever accomplished. While the UFO hobbyists gratefully accepted such people (and instantly elevated them to the questionable status of "famous scientist" because they held a Ph.D.), they soon turned upon their newly found heroes, or splintered into factions of support and dissent.

From kindly old Hermann Oberth to Dr. James McDonald, there were cries of joy, screams of anguish, and finally grim disillusionment. Even the National Congress of Scientific Ufologists, a prominent hobbyist group, proudly awarded Dr. Edward U. Condon a plaque as "Ufologist of the Year" before his notorious Air Force-sponsored anti-UFO report was published.

Since that faux pas, this group has wisely issued their annual award to members of their inner circle.

Dr. J. Allen Hynek, after years of being happily embraced by the true believers, is currently under fire because his Center for UFO Studies has failed to solve the mystery. Dr. Hynek, an astronomer by profession, has been a perennial UFO amateur since the late 1940s, when the Air Force hired him to find astronomical explanations for flying saucer sightings.

Like most scientists-turned-amateur, Hynek has established a record of increasing vagueness and indecision. In the 11 years since he abandoned the Air Force's anti-UFO line and frolicked through the emotional minefield of amateur ufology, he has alternately come out for and against every possible theory and avenue of approach.

Ironically, the man who deserves the most recognition in the UFO field has been systematically marginalized by the ufological establishment. When Professor David Michael Jacobs recently wrote a book purporting to be the complete history of the UFO controversy in America, he managed to put together 332 pages that named this man only once – and then only in an unflattering quote.

Dr. Edward Condon's massive 900-paged boondoggle likewise ignored him. The average UFO potboiler rarely mentions this man. Readers are led to believe that ufology has always been centered on the half-dozen correspondence clubs (MUFON, CUFOS, etc.) and Major Donald E. Keyhoe's long-running battle with the Air Force.

Yet 20 years ago, one name towered above all others in ufology – a name so potent that Capt. Edward Ruppelt of Project Blue Book once publicly credited him with having started the entire UFO controversy. At the very least, he kept the subject alive during the dark days of scorn and ridicule in the 1950s. His name is Ray Palmer.

Despite a serious physical handicap, Palmer's brilliance enabled him to rise quickly in the editorial hierarchy of the then-huge Ziff-Davis publishing company in the 1940s. As editor of *Amazing Stories*, he was the very first professional to recognize the existence of the UFO phenomenon, and he was publishing extensive articles and stories about it years before Kenneth Arnold's historic sighting in 1947. The letters-to- the-editor column of his magazine was always filled with intriguing reports from readers.

It was Palmer who encouraged Arnold to visit Tacoma, Washington, in 1947 and investigate the fascinating Maury Island Incident, a landmark case that was undoubtedly the most important single event in ufology (even though the Air Force later tried to explain the whole episode away as a hoax).

In 1948, Palmer boldly left Ziff-Davis to start his own magazine. From his writings during this period, it is obvious that he knew more about the flying saucer phenomenon than any other living man. He had poured over thousands of reports from his readers, and had initiated several important investigations.

His influence among the growing bands of UFO hobbyists was awesome. Early newspapermen and professional writers leaned heavily on his expertise, but the Air Force intelligence teams ignored him, turning, instead, to a battery of overpaid scientists who squandered tax dollars in a futile search for mundane explanations.

The first issues of his new magazine made it clear that Palmer was very aware of the psychic-occult connections and the importance of the humanoid reports. Yet more than 20 years would pass before the ufological establishment would catch up with him.

The correspondence clubs and amateur newsletters chose to assume a negative stance of their own, denouncing the psychic factors and deliberately suppressing the innumerable occupant reports. It remained for the more objective and open-minded European researchers to open this can of worms.

By the late 1950s, most of the professionals had abandoned the UFO field, because of boredom or disgust with all the childish infighting. Palmer's magazine struggled on as the only national journal on the subject. The correspondence clubs, misled and floundering, ran out of targets for their animosity and turned against him.

His growing preoccupation with the occult and his rejection of the extraterrestrial hypothesis further alienated him from the "nuts and bolts" brigade, who were solely concerned with proving the existence of extraterrestrial spaceships and some massive governmental conspiracy.

Scientists-turned-amateurs drifted in and out of the field, usually lacking the creativity to find ways of applying the coveted scientific method to the elusive UFOs. Like all the other UFO hobbyists before them, they became embroiled in petty personality clashes or became mired in their own conspiracy theories.

The outrageous debacle of the Colorado University UFO study of the late 1960s became a classic example of the kind of churlishness and ineptitude that professorial types can bring to the subject.

Ray Palmer was overshadowed, not by greater minds or more competent investigators, but by a complicated propaganda campaign unwittingly launched by ego-driven true believers.

His following has steadily diminished. His name has been erased from the history books, and his major contribution to the early days of ufology has been consciously reduced to a random footnote or two. Professor Jacobs' revisionist history of the controversy has selectively emphasized the unproductive nonsense of the correspondence clubs and the posturing of the self-styled leaders, who spent most of their time glorifying themselves, while serious UFO investigations remained frozen in a state of total paralysis.

Thirty years have passed since Kenneth Arnold flew into Tacoma and "flying saucers" entered the modern vocabulary. Today, the "crackpot" ideas of Ray Palmer have gained new respectability and acceptance, although various amateurs, both scientific and civilian, are now claiming some of his ideas as their personal "discoveries."

Sadly, ufology is making many of the same mistakes as the professional parapsychologists.

The ufological establishment is now tentatively covering old ground, ignorant of the fact that pioneers like Palmer carefully examined the same things a generation ago. Inadequate and legally discredited tools, such as hypnosis and polygraph tests, are now preoccupying modern investigators.

The rapid worldwide growth of landings, occupant sightings, abductions, and hostile contact cases are still not receiving the attention they deserve. Personality conflicts still run high. At least two recent events, both widely publicized (the Travis Walton episode and the Pascagoula incident) were terribly mishandled by the amateur investigators who became involved.

We can now take a serious retrospective look at the history of UFOs in the past 30 years. We can assess the progress and measure the setbacks. We can analyze the personalities of the past and study their horrendous mistakes.

Above all, we should question former methodologies and try to improve upon them in the future. It has been proved again and again in the past 30 years that money – tax dollars – and science cannot make a significant contribution to the solution of the mystery.

Something else is needed: a bold, imaginative application of deductive reasoning.

Science has failed us because the UFO phenomenon seems to lie outside the tightly drawn boundaries of contemporary science. Almost *any* theory seems to "work" in ufology, because the UFO phenomenon is a mixed bag of the psychic and occult, the psychological and the physiological, the ridiculous and the sublime.

Other hobbies, such as stamp and coin collecting, have solidly established methodologies, outstanding authorities and literate, sensible newsletters. But the ufological establishment is founded on perverse emotionalism and narrow-minded amateurism.

Any serious newcomer to the field finds that he, like author Ralph Blum, must go to Europe and interview the authorities there to gain some insight into the true picture.

He might also find it fruitful to journey to Wisconsin and talk with Ray Palmer. But if he merely plunges headlong into the correspondence clubs and wallows in their often-biased newsletters, he may find himself as confused 30 years from now as he was at the beginning.

He will have become a perennial amateur, climbing a mountain of speculation in the hopes of finding a molehill of fact.

CHAPTER 28

CAN SCIENCE AND SCIENTISTS HELP? – OCTOBER 1977

When Sir Martin Ryle and his team of radio astronomers first detected radio signals from pulsars in 1967, they held an excited debate among themselves. Initially, they speculated they had intercepted "a navigational beacon, fashioned by an extraterrestrial race," and they worried about what course to take. Should they tell the press or the government, or send a note to *Nature* magazine?

"No, the news might seep out and create a public panic, of a War-of-the-Worlds type," a professor said. Fortunately, they decided to keep their discovery a secret, and soon found that the signals were natural in origin, rather than technological.

But the lesson from this episode is clear. If any scientist anywhere should ever actually stumble upon genuine evidence of an extraterrestrial civilization, he would, in all likelihood, keep his finding a secret. Ufologists would be among the last to know.

The scientist would check and recheck his discovery, perhaps for years, and eventually enlist the aid of a few trusted colleagues. In time, he might publish an obscure and obtuse paper, reducing the event to a few mathematical formulae. Then, he would become the center of a controversy, thus risking whatever reputation he might have – for science is dominated by egotistical administrators, and, alas, outright crackpots.

Science is more an application of the known than a pursuit of the unknown. Charles Fort's barbed criticisms of the scientific establishment of his day still hold true – so true we can seriously question the usefulness of scientists in a study of the UFO phenomenon.

As I mentioned in our last issue, chances are that if a large number of established scientists became embroiled in UFO research, they would generate more controversy and personality conflicts than any of our hardcore amateur UFO groups. We already have some outstanding examples.

The scientists and scholars organized, by Colorado University, into the Condon Committee very quickly polarized into two conflicting groups. Within a year, they had lost sight of their contractual goal, and were engaged in hopeless infighting, which ultimately destroyed the whole purpose and worth of the Colorado UFO project.

Two outside scientists, the late Dr. James McDonald and Dr. J. Allen Hynek, later devoted incredible effort to discredit the Condon project. Others, notably Philip Klass, an aerospace writer, labored unduly to attack and discredit McDonald and Hynek. Dr. McDonald spent his last days painstakingly re-investigating cases listed in the Condon Report, while Dr. Hynek used a large part of his long-awaited book to rehash the whole Colorado mess.

Dr. Condon, whose scientific reputation far outweighed that of Hynek and McDonald combined, got in a few licks of his own, in his speeches and public statements. The whole affair developed into a bitter and largely pointless conflict, comparable to Major Keyhoe's campaign against George Adamski in the 1950s.

Similar discord had occurred in the U.S. Air Force in the 1947-55 period, just as the various amateur UFO organizations and publications splintered into dozens of factions, all antagonistic to one another. These battles have kept UFO research in the U.S. in a state of "sleep paralysis."

My first encounter with the scientific community came in the mid-1950s, when archaeology was one of my chief interests. I met, interviewed and befriended a number of prominent archaeologists and Egyptologists, and was soon concerned over their conflicting interpretations of basic facts, and the rather silly feuds and controversies in which they were entangled.

Later, I discovered these same problems permeated every scientific discipline.

As a science editor for Funk & Wagnalls, a large publisher of encyclopedias, one of my tasks was to edit the contributions of scientists. The company called upon leaders in every field to contribute to their books. Only top-ranking physicists, chemists, astronomers, etc. were asked to submit articles.

I was frequently appalled and frustrated by the overall quality of the papers submitted by these distinguished savants. Many bordered on illiteracy. When I tried to find a genuine expert on meteors, I found that astronomers were just as weird, confused, and egocentric as archaeologists.

After a go-round with nuclear physicists from the Atomic Energy Commission, I began to question their maturity, too. (Indeed, the history of the development of the atomic bomb graphically illustrates the naiveté and philosophical confusion of the men who engineered that feat.)

More recently, I spent a year in Washington, D.C. as a special consultant to a large government agency primarily concerned with medical and psychological problems (the Department of Health, Education, and Welfare). There I had daily encounters with all kinds of doctors, psychiatrists, radiologists, and other assorted scientists. So, my personal experiences with science and scientists are both broad and detailed.

Early in my UFO research, I openly questioned the government's practice of calling upon astronomers such as Dr. Carl Sagan for UFO consultations, when the problem seemed to be largely a military and legal one, rather than an astronomical one.

If the UFOs were, in fact, manufactured vehicles, they were openly violating our air space (a military problem), landing illegally in farm fields (a problem for the Federal Aeronautic Administration), and openly harassing citizens by pursuing automobiles, etc. (a problem of ordinance violation – the province of the Federal Bureau of Investigation).

Obviously, none of these agencies were really concerned with the subject, and the Air Force effort was largely a public relations ploy. Apparently, the government decided, in the early 1950s, not to take UFOs seriously on a public level.

Instead of building a small task force of qualified investigators intelligence personnel, psychologists, and scientists trained to interview people in depth, the government established ad hoc committees of astronomers and interested laymen – an approach that could only lead to negative results. And even then, no UFO event was investigated as thoroughly and as systematically as a routine meteor shower, or the discovery of a bit of bone in an old tar pit.

Dr. Hynek was clearly aware of this problem, and frequently stated in interviews that UFO events should be given the "FBI treatment." (The FBI was, in fact, peripherally involved in a few UFO investigations; but when I asked to review the FBI's UFO files in 1967, I was told that no such files existed.)

Of course, the ET buffs speculated for years that the government was hiding some "truth" from the public, assuming that if any real proof was ever found, the Air Force would keep it as secret as Sir Martin's pulsar signals. Yet, knowing how the government operates, and being on intimate terms with many top officials, I found it puzzling that there wasn't even any real rumor of such a discovery (outside the wild ramblings of the ufological press).

The big question is: if we enlist the aid of modern science in UFO research, what kind of scientists do we approach? Dr. Hynek has been talking about his "Invisible College" of scientists for many years now. Very few members of this body have surfaced. We have had more than our share of astronomers and "exobiologists" pontificating on the probabilities of life existing elsewhere in the universe. But that has little, if anything, to do with the real UFO problem.

The real problem, as Dr. Hynek himself keeps stating, is to study the witnesses who have these experiences; that is the logical first step to a real UFO investigation. Once we have established that our major UFO events are caused by an outside stimulus, we can proceed to the second step: the study and interpretation of that stimulus.

The problem thus becomes identical to the problem faced by parapsychologists and psychic investigators. Ufology becomes a behavioral study. When I first pointed this out in Britain's *Flying Saucer Review*, I was subjected to the animosity of many UFO groups, because it was a radical departure from the unproven and unprovable, yet always popular, extraterrestrial hypothesis.

If ufology succeeds in attracting larger numbers of scientists to the fold, what can we really expect?

First of all, the subject offers no profit, and not even an opportunity to win a large government grant. Few, if any, major scientists will be interested. More than any other group, scientists are very concerned with publicity. The right kind of publicity can lead to fame, fortune, and the Nobel Prize. But being associated with any fringe subject can be very detrimental to a scientific career. (Even my own career as a professional writer has suffered greatly because of my connection with UFOs.)

Ironically, Dr. Condon was the most prominent scientist to enter the UFO fray in these 25 years. But he was an exception in many ways, since he had also lent his name to many unpopular causes. He became the subject of so much abuse and ridicule that he was forced to become very negative and defensive soon after the Condon Committee got underway. Other leading scientists will see him as "an example" and will avoid the subject, not wishing to repeat his experience.

This will leave ufology with a cadre of scientific second-stringers for some time to come. Some of them will see ufology as a means for gaining publicity and promoting a flagging career (although such publicity will have an opposite effect – as they will soon discover). Others, those with the fewest qualifications for dealing with the many hidden problems in UFO events, will blunder into the field and serve only to add to the confusion and controversy.

The petty arguments of the UFO journals are already spreading to some of the scientific journals. Phil Klass denounced the Socorro, New Mexico landing as a stunt to promote tourism. Dr. Hynek found Socorro so baffling (after 17 years as a UFO consultant!) that he asked the Air Force if the object wasn't really a secret test vehicle.

New scientists lured into ufology will have to start from scratch, since even at this late date, very little scientific data has been published on the subject. They will have to go through all the bewilderment and theorizing of the amateur newcomers. They will have to learn to separate obvious psychic phenomena from possible UFO phenomena; often, the line is so fine, it is almost indiscernible.

Every scientist who dares to enter the UFO field will have enemies who will delightedly attack him and his new interest at every opportunity. If he does come up with some important new piece of evidence, he may feel that he has to sit on it for years – or forever.

The pitfalls far outweigh the slender advantages in becoming a scientific ufologist. And what would be the point? The scientific community is already capable of generating more controversy, nonsense, and vituperation than any of the UFO organizations.

CHAPTER 29

THE SENTINELS – DECEMBER 1977

"A report comes from London that an officer in the American army stationed at Fort Omaha has worked out an electrical invention that would stop any aerial engine, and bring an aircraft to the ground. The report states that the machine, the details of which are carefully guarded, will project through the air a column of electric energy of almost any desired strength, at any given object, for a distance of many hundreds of yards, the shock of which would render helpless any persons in the aerial craft, and stop its engines."

The above is documentary evidence that the U.S. has developed an EM (electromagnetic) ray capable of stalling engines in the grand manner of flying saucers.

There is just one small flaw in this startling report: It was published in *Popular Mechanics* in September 1909!

Obviously, the London report was merely a wild rumor, since we never heard of that "officer" or his invention again.

Phantom inventions are one of the old, familiar songs of Forteana.

In his last book *Wild Talents*, published in 1932, Charles Fort offered this tantalizing item from *The New York Times*, Oct. 25, 1930:

> About 40 automobiles were stalled for an hour on the road, in Saxony, between Risa and Wurzen. About 40 chauffeurs were probably not voiceless in this matter; and if the German government were experimenting with "secret rays," that was just more of its public secrecy.

In the *Times*, October 27th, was quoted the mathematician and former Premier of France, Paul Painleve: "No experiment thus far conducted would permit us to credit such a report, nor give any prospect of seeing it accomplished in the near future."

Hitler did not rise to power until 1933, and it is very unlikely that any such experiments were going on in 1930. Germany was in ruins politically and economically at the time, and very little experimentation of any kind was taking place.

However, in the spring of 1936, there was a wave of mysteriously stalled automobiles on the roads around Ostia, Italy. The events received extensive newspaper coverage at the time.

Rachel Mussolini, wife of the Italian dictator, was a passenger in one of the inconvenienced cars. Farmers in the area complained to authorities that their sheep were dropping dead, in large numbers, in their fields at the same time. After World War II, it was revealed that Marconi had been experimenting at Ostia in 1936, and had been responsible for these curious effects. He died in 1937; obviously neither the Italians nor the Germans were ever able to utilize his discovery.

Nevertheless, there were universal rumors about mysterious auto stallings throughout the 1930s, particularly in Germany, but also in Great Britain. Our source for this information is none other than the former Director of Intelligence for the Air Staff of the RAF, R.V. Jones. In a lecture before the Newcastle Astronomical Society in 1968, he stated:

> The years before 1939 were filled with stories about an engine-stopping ray. As I heard the story in 1937 or 1938, it was that an English family on holiday in Germany would be traveling in a car when its engine would suddenly fail, invariably on a country road, and usually at the edge of a wood.
>
> A German sentry would then step out of the trees and tell them that there were special tests in progress and that they would be unable to proceed. Some time later, he would come back and tell them that it was all right for them to start the engine again, whereupon they would easily restart the auto and drive off.

Similar rumors sprang up in England. "In one instance, said to have occurred on the Salisbury Plain," Jones continued, "it was no ordinary family that was stalled in their car, but a family of Quakers – well known for telling the truth."

His conclusion was that the rumors grew out of the harmless testing of a television station in Frankfurt, Germany, many hundreds of kilometers from Wurzen and Risa; a very dubious explanation. There were plenty of bizarre electromagnetic effects on the Salisbury Plain in the post-1947 era. Intelligence experts, like scientists, abhor the unknown and the inexplicable, and since the Germans obviously did not have a device that would stall auto ignitions, all such stories had to be pure fiction.

Mysterious electrical failures took a new turn in 1944 when they became a standard gimmick in pulp science fiction. A magazine called *Amazing Stories* began running hoary space tales that included almost all the features of modern UFO reports, including abductions, amnesia, extraterrestrials rushing to Earth to investigate our sudden nuclear explosions, and mysterious rays that could stall autos and tamper with telephones.

Readers flooded the magazine's offices with letters claiming that the stories were true, and that they had had personal experiences with such rays. Editor Raymond A. Palmer began a serious study of these matters, and filled his magazine with the letters and supporting nonfiction articles.

In September 1946, an engineer named W.C. Hefferlin published a piece in *Amazing Stories* claiming that a "circle-winged plane" had been successfully tested in San Francisco in 1927. In June 1946, an ex-Army pilot described his strange experiences in a cave in India, where his companion suffered "a hole the size of a dime in his right bicep ... it was seared inside." (A laser beam?) He signed the letter "A.C.," but a year later, he would be revealed as Fred Lee Crisman.

Richard Shaver was the star of *Amazing Stories* in those days, with his stories of the Dero, a race of mutants who lived deep in caverns and controlled the world through their rays.

An item on the Shaver Mystery in the June 1946 issue contained this bit of intelligence:

> Mr. Shaver wrote that he'd been told by a cavewoman that a Dero meeting under London and Berlin had been held to determine what to do about us. Our editor (Ray Palmer) was to be investigated.
>
> One result of this meeting was a plot to kidnap both our editor and Mr. Shaver, together with our entire families. And to cover up the kidnapping, trained doubles for all of us were to be substituted, and the world would never know that we had been kidnapped and Deros substituted in our place.

This was the first modern reference to the "clone" rumor – a rumor that is still circulating and enjoyed a new revival in 1977.

Early in 1947, *Amazing Stories* adopted a bold subhead, "Extravagant Fiction Today – Cold Fact Tomorrow." Without realizing it himself, Ray Palmer was rapidly becoming one the world's greatest authorities on unidentified flying objects.

From the thousands of letters he was receiving, he was learning about unexplainable power failures, strange cases of brainwashing and amnesia, and mysterious objects seen in the sky and the sea. (One reader, a diver, claimed that in 1935, he had retrieved a strange cylinder from the Pacific Ocean, which contained a window and strange instruments. Metal experts couldn't penetrate it with drills, acid, or dynamite.)

Palmer had been immersed in this fascinating phenomena for three years before UFOs exploded into the headlines in June 1947 and Kenneth Arnold coined the phrase "flying saucer." You can imagine Palmer's excitement when the first UFO reports began to appear in the national press. To him, and to his readers, this was proof that all the seemingly outlandish things he had been publishing were true. He and his authors were exonerated by actual events.

Also vindicated were the innumerable pre-1947 reports of strange objects observed in the skies, and weird manifestations on the ground. The auto stallings in the forests of Germany may have been a symptom of something much less commonplace than electronic testing.

We now know, thanks to the work of researchers like Lucius Farish, that mysterious aerial objects have been cavorting about for hundreds of years. In the wreckage of one of the "ghost-rockets" that exploded over Sweden in 1946, scientists found a peculiar little tube containing "a miniature checker-board." Today we might recognize it as a "chip" – a miniaturized circuit like the ones we now use in computers and electronic gadgets. But chips and transistors were unheard of in 1946.

In the early 1900s, dirigibles and airplanes only slightly ahead of our own designs were seen throughout the world from Sweden to New Zealand. In the 1940s, we were at least thinking of building circular aircraft (though the Navy's "flying flapjack" and the AVRO flying disc both proved to be dismal failures).

We had been contemplating the idea of electronically interfering with ignition systems since 1909, but somebody else had one in operation in the 1930s.

It seems to be a natural progression. Now that we have visited the moon and are looking toward the planets and interstellar travel, the phenomenon is still just one step ahead of us, borrowing ideas from our collective subconscious mind and urging contactees to warn us about atomic bombs.

Perhaps they – whoever they are – are not so paternally concerned with our own destruction. Perhaps if we blow ourselves up, we will be destroying their world, too. That was the warning of Richard Shaver and Ray Palmer in 1945.

Perhaps we share a world, or parallel dimension, with entities that have the insight to see mankind's inherent self-destructiveness and the wisdom to fear it.

CHAPTER 30

SKYQUAKES AND UFOS – JANUARY 1978

Eighty years ago, late in the 19th century, unidentified flying objects made conventional sounds as they flounced and frolicked above American cities. They chugged, clanked, rattled, and putt-putted like ordinary machines of the period, while their mysterious occupants sang songs and played dance music.

But 50 years later, around 1947, the chugging stopped, and weird science fiction-like noises were introduced. Modern flying saucers began beeping their way across our skies, while their mysterious innards whined with high-pitched squeals that sent dogs, cattle, and horses scurrying to protect their hypersensitive ears.

In some cases, these strange objects have offered an entire symphony of surrealistic sounds, ranging from rocket-like roars to the eerie plopping of invisible raindrops.

Just as the blazing rays (some of them quite dangerous) from UFOs provide real evidence of their exact nature and enable us to scale them within the known electromagnetic spectrum, so, too, do their sounds provide us with interesting clues. An analysis of these noises gives us some unexpected insights into the hidden purposes of the objects.

Modern science does have a thorough understanding of the sonic spectrum, and how sound at various levels or frequencies can affect human beings. Soundwaves can put you in a hypnotic trance, instill overwhelming fear, and even kill you. In many documented incidents, UFOs have apparently employed beams of sound for all these effects.

Dead animals found at UFO sites had blood coming from their ears, noses, and mouths – a sure sign of concussion (a sudden, intense change of air pressure), and also a sign of heavy sound waves.

Skeptics of the UFO phenomenon enjoy pointing out that the objects fail to create sonic booms as they dash through our atmosphere at speeds exceeding the speed of sound. Actually, there are many cases in which the UFOs were accompanied by deep, bone-jarring rumbling sounds, and mysterious "skyquakes" (thunderous explosions in the sky) have been recorded for centuries without explanation.

The object that dropped a Canadian newspaper at the feet of Daniel Gray in Burton, Michigan on October 5, 1896, was said to be rumbling rather than chugging through the skies, somewhat out of character with the other strange "airships" that haunted America in 1896-97.

The trick of dumping mundane garbage in their wake – in this case a Canadian newspaper – is an old one, and one that the UFOs have used with great success for many years. By leaving ordinary, earthly trash in their wake, they manage to confound the eager "evidence" collectors and reinforce the skepticism of the nonbelievers.

It is now obvious to leading ufologists everywhere that flying saucers employ every gambit in the psychological warfare rulebook. Their ploys are chiefly aimed at disguising their real nature and concealing their mysterious purposes from us.

If all UFOs looked alike and sounded alike, we would have instant evidence of their reality. But, just as their appearances are changed from sighting to sighting, so, too, do their sounds change. If rumbles and skyquakes accompanied every single sighting, we could be sure they are displacing great masses of air just as supersonic aircraft are supposed to do.

If all UFOs made noises like jet engines, the military authorities would have panicked long ago. They would have been convinced that alien aircraft were actually invading our airspace, and they would have reacted in the classic manner. The task of interpreting the exact nature, origin, and purpose of the objects would have been handed to a secret government agency.

While a thorough investigation was being made, other agencies, such as the FBI, would have been employed to thwart all civilian investigations. Enthusiasts such as Donald Keyhoe, Coral Lorenzen, and Gray Barker would have been jailed on trumped-up charges or shipped off to mental institutions, and magazines such as this one would abruptly have disappeared from the newsstands.

Although there was a crude coverup in the 1950s, it appears, in retrospect, to have been merely another example of bureaucratic bungling, not an all-out attempt to study UFOs and withhold information from the public.

If seeing is believing, so is hearing when it comes to unidentified flying objects.

The phenomenon itself has so many built-in contradictions that most of the confusion was caused by the UFOs themselves, rather than by some sinister government agency. It now seems likely that the government and Air

Force investigations in the early post-1947 period bogged down in the same kind of bewilderment and intramural squabbling that has paralyzed civilian research for so long.

Anything that discharged Canadian newspapers and old shoes, while making supersonic noises at a time when supersonic aircraft were rare or nonexistent, was obviously a hoax, a mistake, or sloppy journalism, according to the reasoning of both sides. Someone somewhere may have expected us to react exactly like that; the success of their unknown missions may have even depended upon such a disorganized reaction.

Witnesses in 1896-97 lacked the technology and vocabulary to describe the modern UFO beeps, whirs, and whines, so the airships manufactured more recognizable noises. When a dirigible passed over Farmersville, Texas on April 19, 1897, witnesses soberly declared they heard passengers singing loudly. A few days earlier, the people in Fontanelle, Iowa, said they heard a phonograph grinding out tinny music as a cigar-shaped UFO glided overhead.

On a few occasions, people were roused from their sleep by strains of ethereal music, and when they looked outside, they saw one of the dirigibles floating past. As in so many modern cases, the UFOs were clearly seeking publicity. They wanted to be seen and discussed, but this tactic may have been pure misdirection. While you watch a magician's waving right hand, his left hand does the dirty work.

We now know that UFOs are not visiting cow pastures and graveyards by chance, or to satisfy some alien curiosity. They are deliberately deceptive. When a score of people see a circular object weaving low over a highway, we can be fairly certain they are witnessing only part of a drama.

Somewhere in the same area, there is usually a man or woman who has been transfixed by the same object, entered a hypnotic-like state and been closely examined physically or mentally by the object. The more casual witnesses to the overflight often report their sighting to the police or newspapers, while the hypnotized witness tends to remain silent.

There are now many thousands of these "silent contactees" throughout the world. Some have had their entire lives altered by a single UFO experience. Their minds have literally been reprogrammed.

Their IQs increase suddenly. They abandon their families and jobs and adopt a whole new lifestyle, often claiming to be on some sort of "mission" to better mankind.

Yet this incredible process is nothing new. It is as old as humanity itself. Many of history's greatest leaders have shared this experience, usually regarding it as supernatural in origin.

If the UFO phenomenon has the power to induce amnesia and restructure the patterns in our brains, then it obviously has the power to manipulate the human race and force us to involuntarily serve its needs and purposes.

Since 1966, scores of eyewitnesses have been closely examined by qualified researchers, and have verified these awesome facts. At the same time, a curtain of mischievous confusion has been created to hide the phenomenon's manipulative powers from us.

There have been meaningless UFO landings staged to support the extraterrestrial hypothesis (ETH). Little men have scurried around like astronauts, collecting rock samples and inspecting garbage cans – while only a few miles away, people were sitting entranced in their cars or homes, having their minds probed by unseen forces.

Gruesome monsters have marched through cemeteries and lovers' lanes, attracting huge crowds of would-be dragon-slayers, while cows have died strange deaths, their bodies drained of blood, in farm fields only a few miles from the monster sightings.

Every true student of the phenomenon is forced to concede that the situation is incredibly complex. The manifestations are so diversified, and the effects so varied, that no single explanation seems applicable. The strongest evidence of all – the medical effects on witnesses – is only now being examined.

It is becoming apparent that *all* paranormal events produce the same effects.

For example, frigid blasts of cold air, or very warm air, are common in monster sightings, cases of ghosts and hauntings, and UFO events. The celebrated EM (electromagnetic) effect is not confined to UFO cases, but also consistently occurs in psychic phenomena.

In episodes involving religious apparitions, we also find the same ingredients that occur in flying saucer contacts. When a human is exposed to a religious "vision," he or she is frequently overcome by a pleasurable sensation known as "ecstasy," which is very similar to a sexual experience.

Eyewitnesses in low-level UFO cases report the same thing – a series of sensations so delightful that they are willing, even anxious, to have repeated experiences with flying saucers.

Medically, religious ecstasy and "UFO joy" are identical. The pleasure center of the brain has somehow been stimulated, either by a beam of electromagnetic energy traversing the nervous system, or by soundwaves.

The simplest form of pleasure induction by soundwaves is music. When musical sounds covering a wide range of the audio spectrum, from bass (low notes) to treble (high notes), are transmitted to our brains, we enter a low-grade form of hypnotic trance.

Music played at a high volume can actually disrupt all thinking processes and produce a kind of temporary ecstasy. Heavy bass notes, such as a steady drumbeat, can actually hypnotize. In primitive cultures, large drums, beating very low on the spectrum in the infrasonic range, are used in religious rites, because they induce trance states and lead to assorted hallucinations and quasi-religious experiences.

In Tibet, monks play low, dramatic tones on long horns, and learn to chant at extremely low octaves, for the same reason (although they also use the low tones to scare away their version of Sasquatch or Yeti, which they call the "Shukpa.")

On another level, music has been used effectively in the brainwashing techniques of psychological warfare. Prisoners exposed to music played at peak volume, 24 hours a day, are, within a short time, reduced to a vegetable state; their minds can then be easily reprogrammed by their tormentors.

The UFO sounds described by witnesses often fall into this "psy-war" category. Eerie whines rising from the infrasonic to the ultrasonic (above the range of human hearing) are often reported, and have even been partially recorded on a few occasions. If these sounds can somehow be adjusted to the specific frequencies of the mind of a witness, a hypnotic-like state can be quickly induced.

The sharp beeps reported at the end of the experience terminate the trance, in much the same way that a human hypnotist brings his patient back to reality by snapping his fingers. The visions seen during the trances might be vividly recalled as seemingly real appearances of ghostly or religious apparitions, or spacemen and spaceships; but, of course, they are purely hallucinatory.

Soundwaves can also produce a much more horrifying experience: extreme, unreasonable fear. Back in the early 1900s, an entire theater audience panicked and fled in terror when an organist accidentally struck notes very low in the bass or infrasonic range. They ran screaming into the streets of London in an uncontrolled frenzy.

Unreasonable fear attends many psychic and occult events. Every state and city has a place where people, and even animals, experience this. These haunted places are carefully avoided; the few people who are brave enough, or foolhardy enough, to venture into them usually quickly return in a very agitated state, not because something horrible happened, but simply because they couldn't stand the "vibrations."

Perhaps there is an old mansion, or swamp, or eerie locale in your own community that has a fear-inducing reputation.

According to innumerable UFO reports, witnesses have been reduced to a state of total terror in the presence of a flying saucer. Their fear extends far beyond the ordinary, and understandable, fear of the unknown. Their hair literally stands on end. Their bladder lets go. Like the British theater audience, they not only flee in abject horror, they refuse to visit the same place again – ever.

It seems as if the UFOs often erect a curtain of fear – of infrasonic sound – around remote forests, swamps, hilltops, and other places where they appear for days or weeks at a time. This same phenomenon occurs in areas where tall, hairy bipeds have been seen. Erstwhile monster catchers bravely plunge into the woods, only to hastily retreat within a short time, like the hardy investigators of haunted houses.

I have had experiences with this fear factor several times over the past few years. My work has accustomed me to prowling cemeteries and other spooky places, alone, late at night. I am not easily frightened, and I certainly can't be frightened by "nothing at all."

Yet I have felt this total, blinding, mind-numbing fear when there was no apparent visible stimulus.

In 1967, there was a long series of strange monster sightings and UFO events in the area of an abandoned ammunition plant (the TNT Area), outside of Point Pleasant, West Virginia. I spent many weeks there interviewing witnesses and exploring the region.

Late one night, I was driving alone along the rutted dirt roads of the TNT Area when, as I passed a certain point, I was suddenly engulfed in fear. I stepped on the gas, and after I went a few yards, my fear vanished as quickly as it came.

I continued to drive, eventually returning to the same spot. Again, a wave of unspeakable fear swept over me.

I drove quickly away from the place and then stopped, puzzled. Why should this one small stretch of road produce this hair-raising effect?

I turned around and slowly headed back, trying to note trees, fence posts, and other landmarks in the dark. Once again, when I reached that particular point, the hair tingled on the back of my neck, and I became genuinely afraid.

When I emerged from the other side of this invisible zone, I stopped and got out of the car. The air was perfectly still.

There wasn't any audible sound – not even a birdcall.

I walked back to the "zone of fear" slowly, alert for any rustle in the bushes, measuring my own breathing and emotions. I was perfectly calm, until I took one step too many and was back in the zone. I almost panicked and ran, but I forced myself to look around and proceed slowly.

By now, I figured I was probably walking through a beam of soundwaves and really had nothing to be afraid of. After I had gone about 15 feet, I stepped out of the zone and everything was normal again.

Now I had to walk through that damned spot again to get back to my car! It was too dark (almost pitch-black), and I was too unfamiliar with the area to attempt to go around the zone.

Although I knew it was harmless, I dreaded reentering it. I actually considered remaining there, only yards from my car, until daybreak. But I finally steeled myself and walked once more through that invisible strip of terror, scared out of my wits yet privately pleased with such an interesting discovery.

In daylight, I returned to the same spot. The zone of fear was gone. I searched nearby power transmission lines, telephone microwave towers, and anything that might have radiated energy through the area. There was nothing.

At other times, in other places, I also experienced this same kind of inexplicable fear. I have seen UFOs myself on a number of occasions, and when they were close enough, this awful fear swept over me again. It was so intense that I couldn't grab my camera to take a picture.

I have also investigated fear zones in other states, but not all of them were related to UFOs. Some were places where hairy monsters had been seen. Some were supposedly haunted by the victims of terrible murders.

In pre-Columbian times, the Indians had marked many areas as "forbidden," because of their fright-inducing vibrations. Some of these same areas remain deserted to this day, bearing names given to them by early settlers – names like Mount Misery, Spooky Hollow, or Devil's Run.

The early post-1947 UFO literature describes the "fear rays" of the UFOs. Those who believe in the total reality of flying saucers might justifiably theorize that UFOs protect their Earth bases by setting up invisible fear shields around them.

I once sat on a hilltop for several evenings, in the Chief Cornstalk Wildlife Area south of Point Pleasant (above Five Mile Creek Road), watching a forest that was bathed in a weird purple light, night after night.

Flying saucers were busy in that part of the Ohio Valley for weeks during 1967, but whenever I tried to penetrate that forest in broad daylight, I was unable to hike more than a few yards. The fear that gripped me there was so overwhelming that I once even vomited as I staggered out.

Another theory that has grown in popularity is that flying saucers may be interdimensional, and that they may be coming from some other space-time continuum, forever beyond the reach of our instruments and telescopes.

They do appear to materialize in specific geographical locations year after year, century after century. These "windows," called "gateways" or "vortexes" by occultists, also produce tales of ghostly apparitions, poltergeists, and bizarre monsters. Many such windows have a long history of disappearances or unexplained deaths of humans and animals.

The interdimensional theorists explain the disappearances as cases in which people simply strayed through some rip in a fourth-dimensional curtain, and blundered into another world that coexists with our own, yet remains separated because its atomic structure is different, and it is in another time frame.

The theory does explain many facets of the UFO phenomenon that cannot be explained by the extraterrestrial hypothesis. But, unfortunately, it can't explain everything.

The deaths in the window areas are as puzzling as the disappearances. There is no satisfactory explanation for the thousands of animals that have been found with their blood drained and certain inedible organs removed, as if by surgery.

However, I have also examined the bodies of dogs, rabbits, and other small animals that were apparently killed by concussion and soundwaves.

I was present one night in the TNT Area, when the air seemed oppressive, and one lady in our party, Mrs. Mary Mallette, suddenly began bleeding from her ear.

A deathray using infrasonic sound has actually been perfected by Vladimir Gavreau of Marseilles, France. It has a range of five miles and is capable of killing every living thing in its path, including leaves on trees. It produces an inaudible soundwave of less than 16 cycles per second, which can penetrate your bones, produce horrible agonies throughout your nervous system, and kill you slowly and painfully.

Sound is nothing but vibrations of the air. A loudspeaker produces soundwaves through the fluctuations of a rapidly moving paper cone. You don't need a complicated technological device to produce soundwaves. Touch a chunk of dry ice with a warm piece of metal and you will get a loud, piercing wail that sounds almost like a human scream.

That very sound, the classic "wail of the banshee," has been heard many times during UFO and monster sightings. As noted earlier, sudden changes of temperature often occur during paranormal events, and it could be that these unearthly screams are produced by atmospheric changes, rather than by a set of weird vocal chords.

Skyquakes, sharp explosions (even the wee fairy folk have reportedly disappeared, suddenly, with a loud bang), and other concussive effects could be an offshoot of the mysterious materialization and dematerialization process.

If an object suddenly materialized in our reality, it would naturally push aside a quantity of air equal to its own mass. This sudden movement of air would produce a sound. When the object left through dematerialization, air would rush into the space it vacated and produce an implosion. Such explosions and implosions are commonly reported in window areas.

Other sounds associated with UFOs could result from beams of light. We know that UFOs are surrounded by ultraviolet and infrared light, because of the many actinic ray burns suffered by witnesses.

We also know that beams of light can produce hissing and crackling sounds. Soldiers sitting far from powerful searchlights have reported hearing such sounds when the searchlight's beam swept above them. Hissing and crackling sounds are frequently reported in UFO cases, along with sounds like the "buzzing of bees." Interestingly, such sounds also occur in religious phenomena such as the "miracle" at Fatima, Portugal, in 1917.

Still other sounds, not so easily explained, have come from UFOs. In the famous Eagle River, Wisconsin case of 1961, witness Joe Simonton said he heard a sound like "tires on a wet pavement." In Jacksonville, Florida, in January 1969, strange clouds appeared emitting sounds "like someone walking on pebbles." Sounds like "rushing wind" and "roaring waterfalls" have also been frequently reported.

Any youngster can create a realistic lion's roar by hauling a piece of string through a tin can, and nearly all of the UFO sounds can be duplicated with modern technology. You don't need a spaceship filled with complicated equipment to produce an ultrasonic whine or high-pitched beep. Almost all of the sounds associated with UFOs are probably the natural result of energy transitions rather than loudspeakers or fiendish radio transmitters.

As forms of electromagnetic energy alter frequencies, they affect our atmosphere in subtle ways. Sometimes they cause temperature changes. Other times, they set up waves or fields of sound. These sounds can never be used as evidence that we are being visited by an alien race from some distant planet, but they can lead us to some concrete information about how the UFO phenomenon is affecting us individually and collectively.

Whether or not these things are entering our skies from outer space or from some interdimensional energy system is really a moot question. It is a question we need to ask.

It is also a question for which we cannot expect an answer.

So many lies and deceptions have been built up around the enigma that we may never find an ultimate solution. "They" are masters of psychological warfare. They can make us see anything they want us to see, and lead us to believe anything they want us to believe.

In the 1890s, everyone was convinced that the dirigibles playing phonographs in the sky were the work of some secret inventor. The dirigibles looked and sounded like the handiwork of some backyard tinkerer, just as the modern UFOs look and sound like what we imagine spaceships from another world would be like.

In earlier times, they posed as angels and devils. In very ancient times, they apparently acted out the roles of gods themselves. But these were all merely disguises; nothing more. While we cursed them, worshipped them, and turned speculating about them into a major intellectual exercise, they continued their mysterious missions – stopping lone travelers on isolated roads to hypnotize them, probe their minds, and remodel their brain circuitry.

Our own psychological warfare experts are now using techniques identical to the UFO tricks. In fact, if we wanted to, we could create our own ufological lore by kidnapping people, subjecting them to these brainwashing tactics, and then turning them loose believing they had visited another planet, or had chatted with a spaceman.

Some ufologists, such as Dr. Leon Davidson, have actually accused the CIA and KGB of doing that very thing. However, such an exercise would be pointless and expensive.

We can only assume that the intelligence behind the UFO phenomenon has a real motive – that a very tangible purpose lies behind all the manipulations of the past several thousand years.

All of the deceptions and disguises are meant to hide the real terror from us. The zones of fear, the beeps in the night, the screaming wails from the swamps, are all part of the centuries-old game – a game so involved and so diffuse that the governments of the world gave up trying to cope with it long ago.

If the UFOs are real, then they have an arsenal far more threatening than our puny atomic stockpiles. They could fill our soldiers with fear, and cause them to throw down their weapons and run for their lives. They could hypnotize us en masse, and while we were all enjoying pleasant hallucinations, they could strip our planet bare.

But if that were their intent, they would have done it long ago.

We might not be defenseless, though. We could use their own weapons against them. They shun – bounce out of the way of – searchlights, so we might be able to shoot them down with laser beams. They are also very sensitive to sound, so we might be able to find frequencies that drive them away.

As mentioned previously, primitive tribes and remote monastic dwellers know that the best way to get rid of demons and abominable snowmen is to blow horns, beat drums, and ring bells. If you want to "spook" a spook, or get rid of a poltergeist, you need only buy a dog whistle – a horn pitched in the ultrasonic range – and blow it when the manifestations occur. Perhaps we could build ultrasonic sirens to defend our cities?

But it is more likely that the weird UFO games will quietly continue for another millennium. Millions of us will continue to be stopped on remote backroads to have our brains tampered with and our thoughts pilfered. We will continue to wake up the next morning with little or no memory of what happened, suffering from the classic UFO symptoms of dehydration, headaches, muscular aches, and lethargy.

Meanwhile our governments and the scientific establishment will continue to tell us that such things don't exist. The UFO enthusiasts will again remind us that the space people are friendly, and have only our interests at heart. They will pass along alien cures for cancer, and notices about the next semi-official "Disclosure" hearing. It will seem perfectly natural and logical when we decide to leave our families and join an army fighting for "truth and justice."

It always has.

CHAPTER 31

THE ENDLESS PROCESSION – JULY 1982

On a warm June evening in 1430 A.D., four peasants in the village of Jaen, Spain, witnessed a remarkable procession. From four separate locations, they watched an estimated 500 people parade along the dusty roads, led by a tall, beautiful woman in a white robe, carrying an infant in her arms.

She wore a glowing mantle, ablaze with iridescent colors casting so much light that it nearly blinded the witnesses. The procession was headed by seven youngsters dressed in white and bearing white crosses, followed by twenty priests marching in two rows, all chanting in an unintelligible tongue. Hundreds of people swarmed behind them, with hordes of barking dogs bringing up the rear.

The procession wound its way through the deserted streets to the church at San Ildefonso, where the glowing lady ascended a silvery throne. Suddenly, at the stroke of midnight, the entire mob vanished, inexplicably, leaving the four amazed peasants standing alone in the darkness. There was not a single footprint or trace of the procession in the dirt along their route.

When they reported their strange experience, the four witnesses were subjected to weeks of questioning and investigation by civil and religious authorities. They had all apparently seen the same identical things, and their report led to the origin of a sacred cult that flourished in Spain for several centuries.

According to the extensive records of the event, one of the witnesses had heard a voice on June 7th and 8th that whispered: "Do not sleep and you will see good things." The procession appeared at 11:30 p.m. on the 10th of July.

Ghostly parades were not restricted to the fifteenth century. In my own investigations, I have heard many bizarre tales from sincere witnesses describing gatherings of strange beings on beaches and hilltops. There have been mysterious convoys of automobiles lacing through small towns in the wee hours, their drivers pale and seemingly entranced.

In a case on Long Island, witnesses reportedly saw "hundreds of dogs, of all sizes and breeds," blocking roads and converging on a field where UFOs had previously been seen.

Oddest of all, phantom police cars and men in police uniforms have appeared in remote places, diverted traffic, and then vanished. During one of their investigative sorties, Ivan Sanderson and his wife were detoured, on a backroad, by a mystery man in a naval uniform.

In a simpler age, the testimony of a solitary witness was sufficient to launch a legend. The thousands of religious miracles, so carefully investigated by religious authorities through the ages, were usually witnessed by one or two people, most often small children. It is probable that a large part of all mythology and folklore has a basis in fact; that a few witnesses actually saw (or thought they saw) the gods or monsters.

In the days before the printed word and electronic media, such incidents were preserved by oral tradition. When a succession of witnesses had reported essentially the same thing, often in the same geographical location, generation after generation, the existence of the god or demon became an established fact. Even the most hardnosed skeptic regarded the cumulative testimony as empirical.

The gods of ancient India and Egypt undoubtedly found life in this fashion, just as Ashtar, Indrid Cold, the MIB, and their various cronies from outer space are now becoming a part of our modern culture.

All of the manifestations of the past have served one primary purpose. They have advanced belief in some theological or philosophical concept, and supported one of the many frames of reference employed to hide the real nature of the phenomenon from us. They engage in what we now call psychological warfare, and they have always exploited our eagerness to believe.

The modern UFO scene is a sociological minefield, because it has produced a worldwide propaganda movement of willing evangelists advocating the existence of people from another planet, who altruistically intend to save us from ourselves.

The leading extraterrestrial *proselytizers* have not had direct experience with the phenomenon themselves. Most have not even seen a funny light bobbling across the sky.

Nevertheless, they are convinced that there is someone out there, and they happily spend all of their time lecturing, appearing on radio and television, and making movies advancing their ideas about the great benign invasion from the cosmos.

There are obviously many grave dangers in this kind of blind belief.

Our studies of the UFO percipients and contactees are teaching us that these encounters are more hallucinatory than real, and that some complex hypnotic process is involved. The real phenomenon is hiding behind a carefully engineered smokescreen of propaganda.

Those funny lights and their hypnotic waves of energy are part of something that is related to this planet, and to us. But that something may be far beyond our meager powers of comprehension.

There are forces that can distort our reality and warp our fields of space and time. When we are caught up in these forces, we struggle to find an acceptable explanation for them, and then the manifestations begin to conform to that explanation, and so reinforce it.

Every few centuries, however, we abandon the old explanations and come up with new ones. Then the phenomenon obligingly tailors itself to those new beliefs. This factor alone indicates that part of the phenomenon, at least, is directly related to the human psyche, and these events are, in part, the work of the individual and collective unconscious.

Unfortunately, another part of the phenomenon seems to be operating outside of the human race (and often beyond time and space), manipulating us constantly, and with impunity. This is the part that we should worry about.

The gods of the ancients are returning, says Erich von Daniken. But actually they have been there all along. While many millions of people have been having casual sightings of strange things in the sky and on the ground, other millions have literally been abducted by the phenomenon and subjected to a brainwashing process.

They emerge from the experience with total amnesia, or with a vague, dreamlike memory or theory about what happened. But their lives change suddenly and remarkably. Their I.Q. is elevated. Their characters and personalities are altered. In several well-documented cases, their chronic ailments have suddenly been cured.

They divorce their wives or husbands, abandon their families, change their names, and move into new and better jobs. The process is more sophisticated now than it was in the time of the caveman, because we, ourselves, are more sophisticated. We have changed slowly, and improved slowly, over those thousands of years.

In other ages, these experiences were regarded as supernatural and mystical. Today, we try to fit them into a technological or scientific framework. Some view the contact stories with alarm, fearing that an alien race is trying to take us over.

One group of ufologists is, in fact, convinced that some of these brain-washed humans have managed to attain top jobs in government and industry, and that the affairs of the world are now being controlled by extra-terrestrial aliens (e.g., Reptilians, Grays, Tall Nordics, etc.).

However, the phenomenon does not really seem interested in our mundane, day-to-day affairs, except where they may influence the mysterious, long-range "plan."

Darwin was partly right, perhaps, when he speculated about a process of evolution, but he did not see it as a completely controlled process. He lacked the historical perspective needed to view the development of mankind as a series of rungs on a long ladder of knowledge and enlightenment. The phenomenon was completely hidden from view in his day, accepted only as the exclusive province of religion or "faith."

The flaw in the "ancient alien" theory is the absence of motive. As it goes, they arrived quietly, gave us some guidance, and then went away just as quietly. Were we just the recipients of an exercise in pure benevolence, or were they *already* making plans for us?

If we really are biochemical robots, constructed by some mad-scientist "Nephilim" in ancient times, we were undoubtedly meant to serve some purpose.

One set of Adam and Eves could not fulfill that purpose. It has taken a very long time, and required the careful conditioning of billions of people.

Today, the nature of that conditioning is slowly being revealed to us, perhaps as a first step toward revealing the entire master plan. The final revelation may not come in our generation, however, or even in the next dozen generations. The phenomenon seems to be in no hurry.

We were first controlled directly by our manufacturers. We called them gods and worshipped them. Before they departed, they set up a system of rule based on "god-kings" – human beings who had been processed and supposedly given hereditary powers not possessed by the general population.

The planet was divided up among about thirty of these god-kings. Their system remained in effect for thousands of years, surviving well into the modern industrial age.

But the mode of control gradually became diluted and polluted by human greed, politics, and religion. Finally, it collapsed altogether.

The legendary conflict between the "serpent race" (those who would enslave mankind) and the rulers of the biochemical robots has continued, however, and the situation is now so desperate that both sides seem willing to expose their modus operandi to us, through overt action in the framework of the UFO phenomenon.

In other ages, we accepted this conflict as a battle for the minds of men. Now, it is becoming apparent that there is more at stake. We, the biochemical robots, are the prize!

The anti-human forces now seem to be *imitating* the real UFO phenomenon, using hallucinations and distortions to confuse us. Meanwhile, the old gods are – science and fakery be damned – trying to reveal more of themselves and their purpose to us.

Millions of people are now able to "see" beyond the visible spectrum and sense the presence of these awesome forces. Our two very different worlds are beginning to overlap.

The future will bring a series of small climaxes, explosions of sudden insights and information, and a gradual strengthening of the communication channels between us and "them." As our awareness increases, we may become more and more subservient to these forces, sliding back to our ancient condition – when they enslaved us.

The process of change is already underway. The UFO phenomenon is rapidly becoming a new religion – a faith based on the premise that we are inferior to some advanced race from another world, coming to rescue us from our own stupidity.

The basic theme of UFO contact has been anarchism – the promise of a marvelous new socio-religious system. It has almost been an election campaign.

The promises have been dazzling, but there has been no attempt to fulfill them. The ancient gods, and their successors, the god-kings, lied to us and manipulated us, and there is no indication that the tactics of the modern ufonauts arc any different.

If we are biochemical robots, helplessly controlled by forces that can scramble our brains, destroy our memories, and use us in any way they see fit, then we are caught up in a poker game being played with marked cards.

Through prophecy, synchronicity, materializations, messages, and other attention-getting devices, someone clearly seems to be trying to tip us off about the marked deck, but we are like the inveterate gambler who, when informed that the game is crooked, shrugs and says, "Well, it's the only game in town."